Until Uhuru

For US Colored Folks

Kommon Knowledge

iUniverse, Inc.
New York   Bloomington

Until Uhuru
For US Colored Folks

iUniverse books may be ordered through booksellers or by contacting:

iUniverse
1663 Liberty Drive
Bloomington, IN 47403
www.iuniverse.com
1-800-Authors (1-800-288-4677)

Because of the dynamic nature of the Internet, any Web addresses or links contained in this book may have changed since publication and may no longer be valid.

ISBN: 978-1-4401-9786-4 (sc)
ISBN: 978-1-4401-9787-1 (ebk)

Printed in the United States of America

iUniverse rev. date: 1/14/2010

To
Kelly for dotting each i
& Renee for crossing every t
through three books now.

Contents

Three

Four

Five

Khamin abu-Jäe

Foreword

Those who speak in the East African tongues of ki-Swahili will inform you that the word uhuru has no literal translation. However, the word uhuru alludes to the concepts of freedom, independence, and liberty. Taken as a movement, uhuru becomes a call for the unity of all Black people from all nations in Africa to come together as one nation for political, economic, and social progress. This includes those of us with ancestors who were displaced through the African Diaspora to distant lands in the Americas, the Caribbean Islands, and Asia. Indeed, we all hail from Africa as her descendants. Here in the United States, it is widely understood that the doctrine of Black Nationalism also involves thinking and acting collectively in order to achieve social, economic, and political gains. So much more than merely a "Back to Africa" movement, uhuru can therefore be seen as being Internationalist in scope. In fact, uhuru can be viewed as the epitome of Black Nationalism whether the people are citizens from Ghana, Namibia, Ethiopia, or Morocco. And so, uhuru holds the same meaning for our brothers and sisters in Brazil, Puerto Rico, Haiti, Harlem, Detroit, and New Orleans too.

Until Uhuru: For US Colored Folks was penned with this very concept in mind. Like uhuru, this book is a coming together of poets, writers, artists, and authors. It is the unification of our observations and our critical thoughts on the state of our union as Black people. With attitudes as diverse as our experiences have been, the reader will note that some of what we say here will not always be in agreement. To the contrary, debating some of the finer points of what it means to be Black in America has become part of the building that we do with each other. So, divergence in our thinking should not be seen as something unconstructive. Like uhuru, the sum of our parts becomes that much greater when taken together as a whole. Therefore, taking as a whole what each of us has to say here makes the message that we share greater as well.

Moreover, there are five tenets which we all seem to agree must be dealt with in order for our people to revolutionize things.

See, our proclamation is a simple one; not only is the revolution being televised but it is also being podcast on youtube and appearing in facebook blogs. And the revolution is being written too- right here on these pages. We have united here and formed a collective of sorts. We do not see ourselves as being any different than the Soulquarians, the Ummah, or the Native Tongues. Their vehicle has been music, however, while this book itself is like a veritable poetic mixtape and each artist has chosen to contribute his or her words in order to touch a much broader audience than any one of us would have been able to reach single-handedly. The world will always know that this is what we feel, think, and believe about being Black in America because we have come together and presented it here. As with the literary legacies of June Jordan, James Baldwin, Richard Wright, Gwendolyn Brooks, and so many others who have left their mark on our world, we too will live on through what we have written. And we will continue to grow and develop as poets, writers, artists, and authors in the same ways that Nikki Giovanni, Amiri Baraka, Haki Madhabuti, and Maya Angelou are doing. Just like many of our contemporaries such as Malik Yusuf, Jessica Care Moore, Ursula Rucker, and Saul Williams, we have something to say to the world. Despite our diversity, Until Uhuru: For US Colored Folks has brought us together from places as different as Cleveland, Atlanta, St. Louis, Cincinnati, New York, Memphis, Philadelphia, and Chicago. And We unite here in the spirit of uhuru; let the people bear witness that we are one.

Maafa

A Swahili term for the African holocaust
in reference to the African lives lost
but justified within their religions;
in the Judeo-Christian tradition
and written about in the Book of Genesis
then corrupted as a thesis
on the Curse of Ham.
Although some considered it a sham,
the common argument was made
in favor of human enslavement as trade.
Just as the chosen Tribe of Judah was exiled from Israel,
its real that chattel enslavement was an entity
of the 17th, 18th, and 19th centuries.
From our brutal abduction,
and the suffering of the Middle Passage,
to being shackled in the slave pen and all,
as WE were kidnapped from places like Ghana, Mali, and Senegal
both post-Civil War and Antebellum.

Now WE must unite until uhuru, so, go out and tell them.

ONE

Acknowledge that it is the system that is corrupt but WE can change it ...

WE are Change

I have struggled with something that should not have been difficult at all: who or what is the impetus for change in a system that is totally corrupt? The answer is simple, the system is corrupt, but WE can change. Our stations in life are not determined by all of the external forces and factors that WE deal with on a daily basis, though I do believe WE are the sum total of all of our experiences, of every person that WE meet, and every conversation that we've ever had. Our mood, our attitude, our dreams, our outlook on life, in general, is determined by our internal barometers, which are gauged by what WE feed our minds. The things that WE want to project: love, self-respect, compassion, sense of self, sense of family, optimism (and the list goes on...) are the things that we want to hold true to, so we have to ingest it to digest it.

While listening to Dave Chappelle recently, in his own way, he opened my mind to how WE truly can affect this corrupt system: know yourself, know your truth, and listen to your inner voices. The system is not responsible for us and it can't tell us who WE are because WE are responsible for uplifting ourselves. Individually, WE need to take our time and have a discourse with ourselves – about who WE are, what WE are, and where WE want to go.

You have to then do what you've got to do for better or for worse, as long as it contributes to the betterment or change of the system. Be fore warned, it may be viewed as socially conscious resistance, to some. You then have to be convinced that it's right for that moment in time. And in knowing your truth you have to understand that the truth is permanent. Your dreams arise from your truth and everything else falls by the wayside- no matter what. Ultimately, our truths should be like music- socially harmonious. In the words of Umar Bin Hassan, you must: "Take your time with the music, for this is for the people. Take your time with the dreams, for this is for the people. Take your time with the revolution, for this is for the people."

Lost @Birth

Some of US may suffer
from Stockholm Syndrome
as WE seek the favor of the oppressor;
an innate inferiority complex from our treatment as something lesser.
And some of US were already lost at birth
with no revolutionary concept of scorched earth.
Lost in this enumerated world of
Octomoms,
Unabombers,
and Trilateral Commissions;
WE get corrupted and twisted with indecision.
To start again,
what the fuck is a "Bipartisan"?!?
It is impossible to serve two masters
but for some reason President Obama believes that he has to
cater to the staunch conservatives'
constituency base while he is serving his.
So, WE can't understand how the same bit of impatience can be
a result of our ignorance and complacency
til the Dummycrats and Republican'ts
divide US, conquer, and cause more trouble again.

White Privilege

What is white privilege in 2009?

Does it mean things are still handed to you based on the lack of pigmentation of your skin?

Or does it mean you don't have to work as hard as those with darker skin to achieve anything?

What does white privilege look like in a capitalist society run amuck by corporate leaders stepping on those who are less economically stable and can't afford the full access pass into Capitalist White American society?

Is Barack Obama successful because he is half white- which gives him a special access pass into the privileged world enjoyed only by white males in the past?

Or, did being financially stable allow him to buy a guest pass for four years?

I ask, is he just another token allowed by the puppet masters to calm the qualms of the underclass, sun-burnt society?

Or am I wrong and white privilege is just a myth; an old wives' tale that mocks non-white Americans?

As people of color make greater gains in this capitalist, –isms filled society,

is the once special white privilege fading to the way side and emerging as a color blind world?

Yes, it may seem like whites still dominate and control America's culture…but do the whites really dominate it, or only those that can afford the admission fee into the top 1% club?

The good ole boys white privilege is being replaced by the super elite capital control society… white dominant, but not for whites-only anymore.

Green privilege is the game of today. If you can afford the entry fee, then you can have a say. No longer does white privilege deny minorities access to mainstream success. White privilege…manifested to divide society by engulfing us in a cloud of racism and hatred is now allowing the true members of green privilege to control and take us all hostage. White privilege… a

parable that has no meaning in a time of lost wages, foreclosures, lost jobs, and Green Privilege. Green Privilege…the new racism of 2009!
If you don't get it, you must have it….and if you don't have it, then I know you get it!

China doesn't have half the resources that Africa has at its command. So how is it then that China could be making such remarkable progress in the world and Africa is left behind as it is?

What has happened is that in China, they had a revolution that was successful in 1949, and this revolution united all of China. China had been divided with warlords here and warlords there, but now under the revolution, China was united.

When England deals with China, it deals with one China. When France deals with China, it deals with one China. When the European Union or the United States deals with China, they deal with one China.

But when any of them deals with Africa, they deal with more than 50 Africas. That is how China was able to be successful while we are not successful.

With all of our resources, we don't even have the ability to have a national economy. We can't have a national economic plan. We can't have a national [...]

I'm reading a [...] that talks about how Afric[...] verse. It said you [...] and somebod[...] peace over [...] truth, and [...] there's [...] ing [...]

co[...]

That's why we have a slogan in our movement that refers to African people worldwide. Touch One! (Touch All!) Touch One! (Touch All!)

I believe that's how it has to be, and if it's not like that then they attack us in these different places and we sit back.

Look at what's happening with Zimbabwe. Clearly, what's happening with Zimbabwe right now is that they intend to make an example and crush that government because they had the audacity to take the land back from those white people who stole the land at gunpoint.

You see that happening, and all of Africa is quiet. You don't hear a single [...] coming from anyb[...] [...]posed to [...]

T[...] [...]t [...]

[...]Afri[...] [...] on [...] Mac[...] [...]nunah [...]Africa is [...]e African

[...]ou can't ge[...] [...]s an African [...] off that same [...]ginia as i[...] [...]t in A[...] [...]of [...]

thing as a Nigerian nation.

The Europeans carved up Africa to suit their own needs. They carved it up in a fashion that of the 48 so-called sub-Saharan African territories, 35 of them have less than 10 million people in them.

How are you going to develop a viable economy and a viable relationship in this world today with a handful of people like that? So [...]

They like to say, "Well look at Darfur." They say in Darfur that 200,000 Africans have been displaced or killed, but in Congo, five million Africans have been killed since 1998.

So how do 200,000 in Darfur rate more significant than five million in Congo? I'll tell you how.

It's because what is happening in Darfur is something that the [...]

UNITE!
until Uhuru

Taya R. Baker

I AM Not Politically COR-RECT

I AM
proud to say
I AM
PO-LI-TI-CAL-LY neutral
I AM
even prouder to say
I put my faith in a THE-O-CRA-CY
though a DE-MO-CRA-CY provides me with certain LI-BER-TIES

Yet, it saddens me
to see the IN-HU-MAN-I-TY
the wanton DIS-RE-GARD
for a man who has WILL-ING-LY
taken the helm of a country that has fallen to, at least, one knee

It dispirits me
to know that even with all of the advances that have been made
HIS-TOR-I-CAL-LY
that one man's worth can still (CO-VERT-LY) be measured by,
not the true content of his character, as we have been taught to believe,
but the QUAN-TI-TY of his melanin – what they see

Forget that he is
    well-spoken
    educated
    exceedingly AR-TI-CU-LATE
    a faithful husband
    a doting father
    a beloved son
(and that he happens to possess a swagger that is reminiscent of a tribal war dance)

Some choose, instead, to ascribe to mis-given IDE-O-LO-GIES
that divide according to race, economics, and ridiculous party BE-LIEFS
They are stymied in their A-BI-LI-TY to grow, to think, to reason IN-TEL-
LI-GENT-LY
to consider that, perhaps, this brown skinned man
with his grace, finesse, and liquidity
has a sincere benevolent civility
for this COUN-TRY that could care less about his guileless attempt to
resurrect their precious
DE-MO-CRA-CY
even I can see that

but then again, ME
I AM
PO-LI-TI-CAL-LY neutral
and
I put my faith in a THE-O-CRA-CY

Henry Charles Griffith, Jr.

Get Up and Go Get It

You hear the drums? ... they're beating in celebratory resonance
Far from pessimist- gleeful and benevolent.
They signify the call to order; a work order manifested.
A resurgence of pride sincerely battle tested and vetted.
A whole new attitude of *get up and go get it.*
The flame has been lit; a beacon on the hill for the entire Diaspora.
The idea that can finally serve as the glue for *all* of us.
The shroud of excuse became increasingly more transparent.
Bigotry and ignorance will always be there, but at this moment they do not render relevance.
We have a man of color as the Leader of the Free World!
Even if the conspiracy of circumstance swirls,
it matters not, because it is the power of the image,
the motor of the takeover, the beginning of the pillage.
This is a period of renaissance- of dream expansion.
A wrinkle in time where you set a goal and *make* it happen.
This chapter in history might not be realized again.
That's why we must recognize that it's *grind time* my friends.

History

The night the world changed I was at home with my children and mother. For the rest of my life I'll remember that night.

Daddy on my cell, yelling how like Jacob, who wouldn't let go 'till God blessed him, he too was holding on until the victory came.

My son, now a man, still believing in the process, waiting with the possibility burning in his amber eyes.

Can it be? A black man like me leading us to trust again? His face spoke.

The U.S. map on the television screen shading red those states that chose the same.

Same mess.

Same lies.

Same fear.

Same ole', same ole' my grandfather used to say.

Waiting on the color of two that held the fate. Ohio and my hometown.

The place I stood with visible pride voting early because he asked us to.

In a long line that wrapped around a downtown city block.

Canvassing neighborhoods with others who traveled all the way from California, Texas, Maine, because the need for change was so great, so urgent.

Pennsylvania the other. The place where the whole democracy dream was loosed. Founding fathers, Constitution, Liberty and Justice for all.

I was taught that in school and I'm beginning to believe it now.

I began to believe it that night.

When those two states popped on the screen shaded blue, votes counted, decision in, I fell to my knees as my instinct demanded.

Thank you Jesus for deliverance,

Thank you for freedom at last,

Thank you, thank you, thank you, thank you, thank you, …

I cried so long, so hard, so loud, so true my voice was gone for three whole days!

But I didn't care.
I just smiled after that- letting my tears fall silently.
Tears filled with the pain of the past released.
Tears filled with forgiveness.
Tears filled with pride.
Tears filled with hope.

Happy Daze?

WE ran away from slave catchers
and WE run away from the law.
Then one of US ran for President.
And he added some color to the White House.
But some of the same double talk came from out of his mouth
while facing the American public and
saving face with the Republicans.
So, there is still plenty of hunger,
homelessness,
and hopelessness
in, this, the Land of Plenty
with the Capitalists' coffers filled
while the Peoples' pantries are still empty.
And there is plenty of racism, oppression, and hate
while WE are expected to just wait
as WE discuss and debate and "Hope for Change"
and our conditions remain largely the same.
Not our be all nor end all;
But WE bet our bottom dollar as if WE were ready to spend all.
Like WE could somehow absolve the American docudrama
by electing Barack Hussein Obama.
So WE can only pretend that happy days are here again
til out come the white robes and hoods to strike up some fear again.
Til WE try integrating new neighborhoods and watch them all sneer again.

No, happy days are not here again.

Education…

Love, peace, unity, trust, and full acceptance of our fellow man
is what we are taught in school.
Hate, violence, division, distrust, and alienation
is what we are shown in our education system.
America's system of education is a double edge blade that continues to handicap
the mild-adjusted, feeble minded individuals of our educated society.
Fifty years after Brown vs. Board, we still have racially separated schools and
black kids being forced to the back of the room (or into special education
dumping grounds). Neighborhood schools or private education, the
unification of the races through education has been a passionate idea that has
no merits.
Why would you want to intermingle, date, live, love, with those whom you
still consider an inferior race of people that you merely allow to reside in the
world of your dominate culture?
Why should I, a Black man, fully accept the embrace of those that I believe
would lynch me and my children for buying a home in their all white
community?!?
Why instill in the next generation that equity is around the corner as long as
they focus on their education and strive to be better? Or do I mean strive to
be white?
Is the education we receive absent of all color? Does it reflect the skin I see
when I look at my brothers?
Education still divides us by not educating whites about our rich past;
forcing us to know all about theirs because they control the curriculum.
When education does discuss our past, it refuses to discuss the future of our
race relations. Malcolm X once said that education is the passport to the
future … well, it must be an invalid passport for us as we are still waiting for
the equal representation.
Education is the alpha and omega of race separation … we have experienced
the alpha. When will we reach the omega?

Got Bilked?

They turned to the stock market
to try to turn a profit
but both J.P. Morgan
and Morgan Stanley
found out how unforgiving the stock market can be.
Just like Merrill got lynched,
WE had to bare Stearns,
and, of course, Goldman got sacked
by mortgage-backed securities
that most stockbrokers were sure would be
worth their weight in U.S. t-bills,
so, whoever thought that there would be bills?
But they paid themselves back with billions in bonuses;
bilked US taxpayers til they ended up owning US.
Like Bernie Madoff
who made off with billions in real estate fraud
and Robert Allen Stanford
who showed US what he stands for
as he bilked billions in a CD scandal.
But as if that wasn't too much for US to handle,
they built bridge funds leveraging
speculated returns off dollar cost averaging
of stocks that lost interest as if they needed Ritalin.
And it left US all riddling,
what the Hell has happened to our economy?!?
See, WE could hear their laughter but nothing was funny
as the Wall Street CEOs laughed.

Yes, they laughed all the way to the bank.
Got bilked?

Satanism is a powerful weapon of wickedness
mastered by those who focus on the evil intent
to wrong others for power, pleasure, pain, and
                    deceit.

The public has been assassinated by lies,
deception, corruption, and greed. The People
have become blind, deaf, and dumb. The Judas
factor is in effect so the Capitalists can make
                    dollars.

            Its a financial massacre.
We see the fangs of the bloodsuckers as they
           smile with vicious intent.

Comrades, watch your backs! The beast is feeding
off of the low class and on the ignorance of the
   righteous. They will fall short before God.

www.com

www and .com
provides US with a world-wide web for some.
A good ole boy network protected
by those of US who are wealthy, white, and well-connected
with bail-outs for Bank of America and Citigroup.
But did the federal government have pity for you
as Fannie Mae and Freddie Mac
fucked US up, over, and back?
Then AIG mistook economic stimulus as need.
Financing more arrogance, ignorance, and greed.
Is it a lack of economics
or just plain old negronomics
providing US with the blueprint
for Black Power
by those of US who lack power?
Peep game and you'll see the same.
WE all play that same sad sounding concerto
anointed in the pain of the ghetto
following the same Judeo-Christian traditions
placing US into the very same strange juxtapositions
of suffering while being estranged
for a lifetime that spans a range
and lasts from the time WE come out of the womb
til WE are returned to the tomb.
Only now capitalistic greed spells financial doom for Wall Street.
Indifferent to whether WE all eat
because they feed off of the proletariat
while only caring if the elite class gets fed.
But no matter if its Communist Red and despite the tactics-
GRASSROOTS REVOLUTION- WE got to get back to it.

Desmond Storm E Jones

Twas the Night Before Our Eviction

(Refugees of the Economy)

Twas the night before our eviction
from our adjustable rate mortgaged house.
No forwarding address,
no 3-month security deposit,
no average Joe the American bailout.

As the stock market just crashed
6 & a half years to the day Joe refinanced.
His non-union job
downsized him to the position
of a hula hoop dance vs. quittin'.
Where there's no more retirement or benefits;
just the benefit of non gainful employment.

As the result, the children grow unaware & hungry
nestled 6 to each bed.
Dreaming of video games, facebook names & basic cable
while the reality of a derogatory credit score-
"who's going to lease to me, co-sign for me, or even loan to me?"
danced inside mom & dads heads.

This stay-at-home mom in her work clothes
knowing the deputy sheriff would be in his cap
with paper work to serve
& day laborers to do everything but observe
just to put us out on our backs.

Like our property to be set on the hedged front lawn.
Snowy day, rainy day, garbage day- it wont matter
AND don't be hurting
miss some tithes at church and
not consistent enough is the
word, message, or sermon
but never the chatter.

Yet over by the window
dad's phone lights up with a flash.
Its a bill collector at 9:01am wanting $350 (not a billion)
or its going to hurt his credit real bad.
"If I had it, I'd have paid it," Joe said.
"The bank sold my mortgage to folk who bet I couldn't afford it.
Don't you understand?"
Joe said, "Mark this to my account next Thursday.
I'm throwing $20 out of my bathroom window and
whoever gets there first gone feel like a lucky man."

Due to economic circumstances what else could Joe say?
The bill collector didn't think it was funny
and hung up just after saying
"Sir, I'm going to mark this down in your report as refusal to pay. See you in court!"
Just then when Joe's stressed posture weighed too heavy; too late to run.
A little ol' deputy sheriff named Nick pulled up
with open hand cuffs and hand by his gun.
Not so lively but this Nick was quick to rub you the wrong way.
He joked, "If this was Israel,
they'd be the Palestinian Movers today!"

"We need a few more days to …"
was all Nick let him say.
Nick pointed back at 8 reasons out of his pocket he does pay.
He didn't even say, "No."
Just, "Step aside or go to jail!"
"Either way- everything gets out today!"

Nick was quick to grab the door and held it open.
To his endeared he implored.

Go slow pay. Or no pay.
You two start upstairs.
On foreclosures. On credit defaults.
You two start in the basement.
Now Repos. Now Refinanced.

Leave nothing in the kitchen but the sink.
Oh! And consumer confidence, you stay here distribute the bags and boxes.
We still got 16 more houses to go on this street.
And then in a twinkling, our ears heard proof.
Bagging, dragging, and evacuating everything under the roof.
Bundles of our belongings covered
the snow covered lawn
from front to back
not neatly or discreetly or like those of
AIG execs.

Bankruptcy while blinking his eyes.
The drill made a dance with his hands
as they removed all the what-knots and locks.
That's when we started feeling the gloomy dread.

This Nick spoke very few kind words
He swore an oath to go straight to his work
Repossessing American Dream-type possessions
like an uncaring jerk!

But I heard him explain
as they drove just out of sight,
"I'll be 10 years or so retired.
The Big 3 will have machines building cars that they can't fire.
They'll be living in pod communities as refugees of the economy
before their credit ratings will ever see the day of light!
They're hiring at Wal-Mart."

I said, "Right."

Case

Sitting on my rack
looking lost in this place.
My Bunkie says to me,
"Why you here- you catch a case?"
"A case! I don't think so.
I just didn't pay what I owe."
He says, "Sounds like that child support shit there bro."
He says again, "This is my third time in the QG.
All because my woman didn't believe me.
You see I've been here for 19 long nights.
I have 11 more THEN there's gonna be a fight."
With the look in my eyes- I was lost- he could see that.
He says to me – "Relax bro because 90% of us is black."
He tells me that most guys are here 'cause they hard and being a thug.
Runnin' the streets for that street money drug.
Slingin' that crack, heroin, or dog and other shit.
Lookin' for that crack head- my bad- he said that *lick*.
You see a lick is a dope fiend.
A power lick- well you get what I mean.
He says to me "I'm here for another reason.
I sling a little bit – but I'm here for teason."
Teason?!?
I'm thinking…is that a word- is he for real?!?
Hey this brother 6'4" and 260- I just said he was for real!!!
"You see most brothers here rather be caught with a gun than a joint.
'Cause with a gun you get probation- with weed 6 months in the joint."
Then my proper ass tryin' to be hard says,
"the system is harder on marijuana than havin' a gat?"
With this brother laughin' at me he says, "Yea- its something like that."
Then he looks real serious- with a glare in his eyes.

He says that "I'm innocent"- MAN that caught me by surprise.

He talks about how he's in here 'cause he caught a DV.

That's domestic violence- I see yall lookin' at me.

He says, "I'm here because I was out all night in the streets with my man named Black …

Just doin' what I do- 'cause my girl loves that Baby Phat.

She didn't believe me so she made a phone call.

Hey…she didn't call me, she called the freakin' law.

They were there when I pulled up- couldn't even get out of my truck.

With their tazers pointed at me, man, I'm thinking what the fuck?!?

30 days and nights in this concrete place …

All because my bitch is jealous, so, I caught a fuckin' case."

Muingi (the Movement)

A Black man screams
from the pain a judge's gavel brings
to his broken spirit.
Spoken on through our lyrics
for the damnation
and the condemnation
of those souls descending;
some into graveyards and others into prisons.
And written for all of those hearts and souls
that remain down in the ghettoes
on the degeneration of the Black race
thru the denigration of the Black race
in an unjust justice system.

Shawqui Y. Novoa

Wall Street II

In the making

In the making of Wall Street

Ummm wall

Wall of a gathering of people

Wall

Wall of control

Wheel of a wall,

Built of our people

Slave to man

Finance of

economic greed

Lust of life

In prison, our minds' generation

of exchange

exchange of our souls

our forefathers, yes this was stress put to the test

Financial gold mine of one self.

Ummm

Comprehensive, yet apprehensive

rape of our self-respect

rape of our economic wealth

rape of our ethnicity

Ummm

Were we

Are we a product of Wall Street?

Wall Street

The Dow is up

trading, trading!

Yes, we were traded

and not given our investment back,

for we paid the highest price

for we were traded before there was trading

we were the numbers on the board

trading, trading!

Wall Street

Yes, we were the making of Wall Street.

Pro pa-Ganda

Has Israel targeted Palestine
abandoning over time
what an accord for peace required?
Or was it Hamas who broke the cease fire?
See, WE ignore what is seen
until it becomes what WE believe
as if Tel Aviv can tell no tales on television.
With indecision from front page reading
of the lies that a false media keeps on feeding
off of the terrorism occupying the Gaza Strip
with weapons smuggled in by the Communists.
Backed by America behind-the-scenes
providing the Israelis with F-16s,
Apache helicopters,
and M1 Abrams Tanks.
Plus the financial backing of the World Bank.
And it seems like propaganda
has become a false media standard.
While Israeli troops
only tighten their noose on the Holy Land,
U.N. Resolutions and the Articles of the Geneva Convention
seemed to be unilaterally ignored with the intention
of targeting Hamas militants
but causing casualties among the Palestinian innocents.
See, "Forgive US our trespasses" when applied in Jerusalem
is applicable to the Jews, the Christians, and the Muslims.

Jennifer 'Jai' Washington

Judgment Day

Silence in this court! Now all shall rise.
We've charged the defendant with deception & lies.
For they've committed a crime that is oh so horrendous…
that I'm sorry to say if ever continuous.
The charges today are not just those listed above;
There's murder, slander, & there ain't no love.
The victims of the crime have yet to recover.
They've been beaten down and abused like a mad-man's lover.
They were denied all the basic necessities of life.
They were robbed of their families: a husband; a child; a wife.
Don't sit there today jurors with blank stares on your face.
This trial is all about hatred, bigotry, & my race.
For the fight for freedom that was long overdue,
was made an experience that no human being should go through.
And so I ask of you, as we present all the evidence of this case.
That you listen to their cries of sorrow and let the souls fill the space.
The space in your heart that's been taught not to understand,
that the color is just pigmentation, but the soul of what is truly the man.
What's that your honor? Did the defense say they object?
Did they say that we're treating their client with very little respect?
Well, I am sorry 'Mr. Attorney' if I seem a little upset,
But you have treated my mothers & fathers with cold, cruel calculated neglect.
You know I thought about this case as I wondered of my ancestry.
I thought of the hellous journey and how hard it had to be.
To be taken away from your homeland; whether sold by friend or foe,
and to realize that all your dreams you will never come to know.
Your family had to separate and all go their separate ways.
So you held them tight to ingrain their memory in your ever constant gaze.
For those who held onto the hope that somehow this could be a better life,

26

they'd soon realize they'd be stabbed by the ever wielding mad-man's knife.
Oh yes, your Honor- let's get to the point at hand…

Let's bring up the current atrocities that still plague the misunderstood Black man.

I don't think I need to go into the history of these cases; I'll just name a few: Timothy Thomas and Roger Owensby are names that should be very familiar to you.

The person of whom I speak is there! Yes, the government and society as a whole.

They portray my client as a savage; a monster without a soul.

But you know what? I commend this People who have survived 500 years of public dismay.

They've endured and continue to thrive and will do so until their dying day.

Not only am I proud to represent them; I include myself in the civil suit.

I am a member of this elite club; of this there is no dispute.

With that, I close your Honor. I leave it in your most capable hands.

For though your names are many (Jah, Yahweh, Jehovah, Allah, Buddha, or Jesus), Your decision will be the only one that stands.

BLESSINGS!!!

Cops Cre-8-Shun

On New Year's Day
in New Orleans,
Adolph Grimes got
14 shots from the cops-
12 of them hit in his back.
Did I mention that he was Black?
And to my dismay
on the very same day
in the city of Oakland,
Oscar Grant was killed by a cop and captured on youtube.com
but his story was barely covered on the news by some.
And remember Sean Bell?
On the night before hearing his wedding bells,
his celebration was cut short I understand
as New York cops fired 50 shots into his van.
Goddamn!!!
Is it open season in Amerikkka on a Black Man?!?
Or do these killer cops
create cop killers?

In Whom We Trust

More voices than choices, more choices than voices. Is there ever a need for a
dialog? As this hung jury type country jogs with shades on in the fog.
Divided? Misguided? Disguised as a break down of communication.
Where climate controlled locked & blocked closets preserve our
skeletons and this nation.
Some will die not admitting. Others resolve by "no benefits" type quitting.
Responsibility while race relations is on extended vacation. What's
the sensation? One man's problem is another man's solution ...
Confucius or confused us? While we gladly complain sitting in the
passenger seat until this country's driving starts to scare us ...
Us? The U.S. united separately on different fronts
different stunts
different views of what the people want.
But how often is that what we need? Who cares if the masses succeed?
In a society where success is gauged and rhymes with greed.
I guess it's easier to deny; pointing the finger at "the other guy". Blaming,
naming, shaming, any point of power they might be claiming ... or
at least until that class action law suit is won. What college teaches
"Get Over It 101"?
We live in a country that to a subscribed few is advertised as a paradise. For
those who no longer fear or believe in what they swear by, human
behavior is some people's savior or marketing tool when creating
another flavor of ... classism, capitalism, racism.
Crazy glued views of how things aren't what they used to be as our actions
contradict thepurpose of time and history.
Time being shaped by our destiny schedules.
History being shaped by **I**, **us**, and **We the People** of the United States of
America. Where

Hate
Debate
and **Failure** to **Relate**
are cubic zirconias for this country's criteria.
Conflict of interest has out-lived its pension and full benefits as well as leaving more voices and less choices; making it harder for who to tell?
Dialog inhibition has the stock market making our country's overhead decision, down sizing from the bottom line
The bottom lives
The lowercased *u*'s
The lowercased *i*'s
trying to keep up with the Dow Jones's ... surprised??
In God we trust taken for granted more than printed. But money makes the world go round with no mention of
God or trust in it ...
As we, the hung jury, find ourselves as the defendants ... **guilty** for sitting on empty expecting full service at a
Self serve **station** in a
Self serve **nation** waiting for a
fill up!
In Whom We Trust

Only Real Here

There will be
no existing
in a dream-state
here.
But ever mindful of these words.
Acceptance and Integrate
here.
Find it hard to keep the faith
here.
So I choose not to
perpetuate
the notion
that hope can stop the hate
here.
Won't pretend
for the pretending's sake
here
that your freedom is not at stake
here
that the fathers of these United States
did not seek to control your fate
here.
Made you forget
that you were once regal.
So here
no delusions of being equal.
That's clear.
President Obama
can only change policy
not people

for real.
Mental imprisonment
has always been at play
here.
And your belief
in this American Dream
keeps them safe.
Stuck in one place
here.
Chasing dollars
but barely getting cents
here.
Keeps you dependent.
Yet wages can't pay the rent
here.
Education insufficient
here.
Quality of life
below the poverty line
here.
Running out of time
here.
But there is no basis
for white folks to feel superior
to African races
here.
Privilege is not the same as superiority.
So they have no authority
here.
No waiting for their concern
here.
Let no more niggahs burn
here.
No identifying
with the deliberate
mystifying of your Blackness
here.
No feeding into
the things they believe
about you
here.

No more
dancing a jig for a dollar or two
here.
The ghetto you were born in
is exactly where they intended
to bury you
here.
But what they do
does not testify to our inadequacy.
Their mastery
of destruction more accurately
speaks to their lack of humanity
and to their inclination towards insanity.
So no making peace with mediocrity
here.
No finding comfort
within the conditions of poverty
here.
No pretending like what we live in
is a democracy
here.
Can't ignore the hypocrisy.
The irony is in the mockery.
Denzel can win an Oscar for his debauchery
but not for portraying Brother Malcolm.
But they can stop the charade
here.
We seek not their approval
nor their accolades
here.
No more bending over backwards
trying to see the sun
here.
No more trying to overcome
here.
And no more running
from America's cunning
here.
Ain't a damn thing funny
here.
No more believing that

being ghetto is equivalent to being Black
here.
No more being unaware of
the strength of the blood
that flows through your veins
here.
No more being left
to drown in floods
and insurmountable waves
here.
We take the reigns
here.
No arms stretched open
towards assimilation
here.
No begging
asking
or waiting
for reparations
here.
No explanations.
No need for validations
here.
One Black groove
for one Black nation
here.
No long debates
trying to rationalize self-hate
here.
No politically corrected language
here.
No giving into anguish
here.
Only real life.
My life.
And yes I talk about
my fight
here.
No shame
for the way I speak
here.

I speak so that my people
can understand me
here.
No walking that tight rope
strung by this society's
twisted ideologies
here.
No anticipation
of an apology
here
for your justification
of the eradication
of Black unification
here.
Your Devil's stones
can't break my spiritual bones
here.
Too Black, Too Strong
here.
You won't find no
house slave
here.
No back breaking
here.
No hair straightening
here.
No corporate oppression
holding me down.
Only forward movement.
Only upward bound
here.
Understand
what I am saying
here.
Yes, I wear my pride on my sleeve.
In fact,
it's right
here
next to my reality
because
here

before I am
Woman, Mother,
Daughter, Sister,
Wife, Lover
Professional
or even Poet
I am first Black
here.
Accepting
nothing less than respect
here.
Won't give what we don't get
here.
Unapologetically
living our lives.
Uncompromised
here.
The greatness in us
finally recognized.
Eyes on the prize
here.
And we
discredit the lies
right now
right here.
You know the deal
here.
It's only real here.

Two

*Change begins with US
learning to love ourselves and
leads to our inner reform …*

Seek Knowledge of Self

Reverend Dr. Martin Luther King, Jr. said, "There is nothing more dangerous than to build a society with a large segment of people in that society who feel that they have no stake in it; who feel that they have nothing to lose. People who have a stake in their society, protect that society, but when they don't have it, they unconsciously want to destroy it."

What will you discover as you translate the meaning of the written text that is before you? Will your senses awaken to discover new meaning of self? Will you crave a better understanding of the world that consumes your every thought in hopes of giving birth to a new you? Or will you just see the words before you merely as something to read, and perhaps to understand, but not to comprehend as America does with so many of those silent screams that cry out for freedom?

A person of color first finds his identify in the family, neighborhood, and community from which he is raised. That identity is forged and strengthened through what he perceives as an identity of self. An identity that he may often question and examine when America's white dominated culture of education, beliefs, norms, values, and morals proclaim that his speech, mannerisms, and culture does not represent the dominate culture. Conceivably, this may force him to accept a position of feeling inferior for not being part of the dominant culture on one hand. On the other hand, conforming and assimilating to the mainstream culture is something else that may happen.

Jamil Abdullah Al-Amin (H. Rap Brown) confirms this, "Racism systematically verifies itself anytime the slave can only be free by imitating his master."

Psychology teaches US that our identity comes partly from self-certainty and ideological values. Regarding self-certainty, identity largely results from how consistent and unswerving WE feel within our self-image and the image that WE present to other people. Among other factors, this is coupled with our set of basic social, philosophical, and/or religious values for living with which WE can agree and identify. Personal conflict and crisis of identity is often the result for the person of color who finds inconsistencies and irregularities in his family, neighborhood, and community while seeking to define his identity within the dominant American culture.

In addition, his assimilation into mainstream views, beliefs, and culture causes him to lose parts of himself; often before he has had a chance to discover certain parts of himself, that part may have already been lost. According to Dr. Asa G. Hilliard: "As a cumulative result of all these things, we have lost our solidarity ... our unity. When we lost our unity, we lost our political advantage, economical advantage, and even our mental orientation. We lost a sense of self and a clear sense of belonging. We also lost a clear sense of wholeness, continuity, and purpose."

And it seems as if that is the way the America wants it to be. As the person of color strives to succeed and leave his mark in the world, he begins playing a game using rules that were designed by a few in order to control the masses; a game that was not designed for many people of color like him to win.

However, it is not enough for US to just acknowledge that the system that is corrupt without also proclaiming that WE can change it. That change begins within US taking a look inwardly and finding out who WE are as people of color. That change continues by rectifying any identity crises and personal conflicts within ourselves; an inner reform of our views, beliefs, and culture.

According to Imam W. Deen Mohammed, "Persons need a perception of themselves and the perception of the reality for them in any given situation."

Having knowledge of self enables US to know exactly what it is that WE stand for along with what WE will not stand for as well. While being tried for conspiracy alongside the Panther 21, Afeni Shakur posed the following question in a prison letter: "Does the state rule the people or do the people rule the state?" WE must answer it by putting ourselves first and redefining the dominant culture in America instead of letting the dominant culture in America define US. This is how WE can begin to change things.

Staci Celeste

Black Beauty

Brown skin beauty, hold your head up on high.
This world formed on your shoulder,
wide, strong, dark shoulders braced to
carry decades of pain, joy, hope, and
possibility.
Eyes like charcoal.
See through to the soul.
Full, round, succulent lips,
blackberry sweet,
tell me your secrets.
Whisper sweetly in the dark, and trust that the darkness
will keep them safe.
Until the time comes that a little black girl cries into the night,
searching for her beauty,
searching for herself,
and finds your wisdom.

CELIBACY

Castrating my emotions by
Eliminating my sexual encounters because
Licking leads them to loving and I am
Incapable of loving them back so I
Bind my desires in activity and
Allow access only to my shallowest parts because
Constant flirtations with mediocrity leave me
Yearning for something that will touch my soul
... So I Wait ...

This Feeling, This Knowing

I cannot contain
this
feeling
this
knowing
that I am enough.
My dreams seem real enough
to touch.
So glad that
shifts in the atmosphere
no longer interrupt
my soul just
comprehends the must
to keep pressing
no matter what the mess is.
Stopped stressing
over every answer to every question
because wherever I'm stepping
God is guiding my direction
and giving me His protection.
Meeting me at every intersection
with a little retrospection
to learn from my passed discretions.
Third eye granted the projection
of the future blessings.
So for the rest
of my quest
I pull the armor of courage
across my chest
and summon much needed

determination
instead of concentrating
on any limitations.
For it is God's expectation
that I will live the full manifestation
of His plan for me
His is the only affirmation
I need.
He says move, I take heed
He tells me to be still
I freeze.
Wave your hand if you feel me.

I cannot conceal
this feeling
this knowing
that I am enough.
I've been
put in touch
with the greatness
in me.
So even when my sight
is blurred
by the water in my eyes
I just look to the skies
and I am assured that
my strength
is not compromised
by my tears.
I might not be the smartest
prettiest
most revered.
But thank God I'm here.
Imperfect but perfectly self aware
of who I be.
From the soul of my feet
to the very tip
of the longest piece
of my hair.
Sometimes
standing in the need of prayer

but I am unapologetically
unequivocally and
undeniably
a Black woman.
Rightfully
sovereign
over my own fate
and on this journey
that I have been called to take
there is more at stake
than how many mistakes I make.
It's about how many steps
of faith
I take.
So I move forward
pushing every regret;
every miscalculated step
behind me.
Staying focused.
Avoiding the ill-represented.
And the grimy
wish they could outshine me.
But God stands behind me.
So from time to time
I have to give praises to the Most High.
Wave your hand if you don't mind me.

How could I confine
this feeling
this knowing
that I am enough?
All grown-up.
Sweet but tough.
Golden to the eye.
Soft to the touch.
You might want to catch up.
See what's going on
over here in my light.
Every poem that I write
represents this life.
Yours and mines alike.

So they are never just rhymes.
I represent you.
Forever striving to
give truth
in every word God guides
me to recite to you.
There will be tests.
Won't always do your best.
You'll earn some A's.
Might earn some F's.
But it's all for the best.
When you realize
that you have been made wise
and comfortable in
your sun-kissed skin
and able to articulate
what you expect
from anyone who shares your space.
If you don't know what it is
that anchors you in place
then you hold onto nothing.
Better find something
to plant your feet in.
Better be concrete
in what you believe.
Wave your hand if you know like me.

I couldn't
even if I tried
hide
from this feeling
because this knowing simply
will not be denied.
Heaven is full of blessings
for which nobody bothered to ask.
My task
has been to believe that
what He has
for me is mine to grasp.
Trust that you shall be given
that for which you have the courage to

speak into existence
because in an abundance of water
only the fool is thirsty.
My mother birthed me
but God qualified me worthy
So no man, or wo-man
or circumstance
can hurt me
or unnerve me.
Try to move me
if you think you can
but my life
is in His hands
and His is the master plan.
So conjure.
Deceive.
Pretend that you dig me.
But no weapon you form
can spin me.
So let the bullshit miss me.
And if you know like I know
and I know that you do
wave your hand
and let me wave mine with you!

Staci Celeste

Woman, I am

Bold, Black, and Beautiful
I am.
Directed from the life source within,
I journey forward.
The fear of the unknown does not hinder me
for I know
that I am not in control.
I have known love and hate,
laughter and tears,
bravery and cowardice,
life and death,
obstacles and triumphs.
Defeat has been the only stranger.
I am a teacher, giver, lover, fighter, nurturer, preacher, writer.
Life bearer to two great ones.
I am a woman.
Woman, I am.

Taya R. Baker

Invisible in My Black...ness

February two thousand and one, one, one...
and it makes me sad and angry
to know, see, think, feel...
that people are still uncomfortable
with my Blackness
my ebony
my skin
my me
my vast amount, quantity
of melanin.
It's unchangeable you know
and, most certainly, unthinkable
to consider that I can be
will be
choose to beee...
anything other than I am.

I can't apologize for, won't apologize for
being me.
I can only apologize for being
disconnected
disjointed
disillusioned
disquieted
disheartened
distressed
disturbed
by a world that is
hating
hateful

lacking love…less
clueless
unthinking
uncaring.
Believing that
when they look at me
thru me
around me
past me
above me
below me
that (it's possible)
I am invisible
in my Black…ness

Look again…

Khamin abu-Jäe

WE BE (the Infinitive)

WE came of age
and took our place out on the corners;
the ghetto changing of the guard.
Young lives lived hard.
Like George Jackson, WE knew nothing when WE were born
but necessity and environment gave US form.

Defining our reality and what it means to BE.

Something that WE must all stand and confess
like the state of our Black union address
or else be prepared to stand and deliver
via cinderblock shoes from the bottom of the river.
See, even the assassinations of Malcolm X, MLK, and JFK
took place under the watchful eye of LBJ.
Conspicuously done and executed overtly.
with our government agencies operating covertly
then acting unwittingly
or with an inability
to locate the guilty assassins
until after enough time that WE forget what has happened.

Defining our reality and what it means to BE.

As Wall Street being bailed out like Geronimo
was more scandalous than abu-Gharib or Guantanamo
facing off the American public and
congressional Democrats and Republicans
like corrupt police who cover-up and attempt to excuse
their fellow boys-in-blue; but that's just what they do.

No matter whether heads first or ass last,
Malcolm X said WE can still die by the ballot or the bullet just as fast.
And Kathleen Cleaver said to put the first ones last and the last ones first.
But WE live our backwards ass lives ass backwards

Defining our reality and what it means to BE.

Curiosity seekers have a look-see
as stockbrokers play the role of bookies
and curiosity kills cats.
Both before and after the fact,
presumed niggas by association;
an affirmation that swallows just as hard
because every Dead Nigga Boulevard
is just a dead-ended Avenue of Dreams.
WE got American made F-16s,
and M-16s,
and M-1s,
and then some
over in Israel.
It sounds like a paranoid conspiracy theory but it's real
and it smells like the same ole foul odor-
a new whirl odor-
as WE flush down into the New World Order.

Defining our reality and what it means to BE.

Like Hip-Hop's prophets
stacking their profits
as their prophecies are stacked 16 bars at a time,
political power can come from a rhyme
and spark a revolution.
Perhaps WE start by burning the Constitution;
it ain't worth the paper its printed on
and ain't worth all the time WE keep spending on
our repeated calls for the civil disobedience and dissident dissent
of revolutionaries, radicals, and militants.
To do is to BE in the truest form of the infinitive.
So, fuck Black people who mindlessly recite their rhetoric
like: "There can be no more excuses."
To the struggle of the People its counterproductive and useless

because although a Black president for the People was given,
he lacks the precedence for erasing the racism
that is so deeply embedded and interwoven
into America's fabric and fibers;
the very fundamentals
and foundations of this nation.

Defining our reality and what it means to BE.

Separated from first class
and then seated last
but more so divided than conquered
because WE can change the world one word at a time;
political power through rhyme.
So, the revolution WE all need
involves verbalizing a solution that WE can all heed.
Proving not only that the revolution will be televised
but the revelations have been prophesized
with a resolution that may be to terrorize
as long as WE are still owed 40 acres and a mule.

Defining our reality and what it means to BE.

Letter to the Black Woman: Who She Is

(part I)

To the earth, a glorious creation well designed by patience and intelligence above mortal standards.

You are a vast product; elite in your sexual cipher that only a god can understand when you go through your positive and negative transitions and personalities.

You are the she, female organism in flesh expressing feminine chromosomes of life.

You are she, wisdom, more than rubies and personal glamour of life's expectation.

You come in many shades, only colors an artist can create as if he were painting.

Sometimes we've been forced into combat with each other to confuse our source of power. But you are my element of understanding possessing the abilities to make man go right or left depending on you and his knowledge of self and your highness.

I love the white robe you wear when you're royally serving God. The way it lifts up slightly when you're kneeling to pray and meditate, honoring God, acknowledging His supreme enlightenment of the 9th council, representing birth.

Stay strong, your Highness, because you belong to God.

Letter to the Black Woman: Birth

(part II)

You are sweetness; the mother of big and small worlds. You are the life giver to physical dominion as if a team of scientists were in you, and they are.

These scientists are the angelic beings, the spirit gems of cosmic glass working through God's essence.

The thought is deep so life came about flowing from God through man, through woman, through God.

We teleport life through you because you are the ancient carrier of time holding the package we men presented to you for delivery.

I saw you before in other worlds before this one. On many other planets and realms. I married you once upon a time in the last galaxy until we passed away in the spirit-ship, incarnating again through the wheel of destiny.

You are the Mother-ship so many talk about carrying them to the next life time. Now you know the truth.

God chose you for the traveling pod of formality.
Creating the young Christs of matter into a message of peace.

Vision and dreams are only memories of what we had seen in your womb Black Queen.

We the People peo·ple (pi:pl) n. pl -ples for 4, v. -
pled, -pling. 1. persons indefinitely or collectively 2. persons, whether men,
women, or children, considered as numerable individuals forming a group 3.
human beings, as distinguished from animals or other beings 4. the entire
body of persons who constitute a community, tribe, nation, or other group by
virtue of a common culture, history, religion, or the like 5. the persons of any
particular group, company, or numb_____ed in combination) 6.
the ordinary persons, as dis_____ve wealth, rank,
influence, etc. 7. the subje_____ruler, leader,
employer, etc. 8. the subj_____uler, leader,
employer, etc. 9. a person_____ossessive in
Communist or left-wing_____tion operates
under the control of or_____er Communist
leadership) 11. anima_____with object) to
furnish with people_____if with people.
Origin: 1225-7_____le < L populus.

Changeling

I used to be
someone else
not physically but
spiritually.

I used to prey on others
use their weaknesses
to get what I wanted
until one day ...
things changed.

One day I bit an apple
with a worm that turned
and my transformation
was borne.

I can't tell you why
that apple
on THAT day
changed my life;
all I can tell you, is that it did.

Now I spend my days
trying to make amends.
If not towards the ones I've hurt
then by helping someone else.

Paying back to anyone
what I would have done to everyone
had I not changed;

had God not changed me.

But I wonder if,
when I meet Him,
will He see the sincerity in my heart
even though I know I will have to pay
for the sins I committed?

And I will gladly pay the price
because I see clearly what a predator I was
but there is a trace of fear-
fear born from knowing how badly
I treated others; mistreated them.

But I move forward
doing what I can to make amends
in this life
before I am held accountable for my wrongs.

And I hope that in the end
my life will show that
once I saw the error of my ways
I did enough good to make peace
with the many wrongs I did to others.

Jäe ki-Moja

Amer-I-CAN

America!
Yes, I CAN
change the future.
I dream like Dr. King,
of rights for African
Amer-I-CANS.
Of black raised fists,
changing the world like Angela Davis.
Saying YES WE CAN!
Like Obama.
Young Amer-I-CANS.
I know I CAN
change red, white, and blue to
red, black, and green.

Ode to the Future

I come to you, Dear Future, with words of wisdom,
as my eyes have seen thirteen thousand and eight hundred sunrises.
This provides great insight.
Dear Future, remember that you are the only one we have.
The only HOPE we have.
Open your mouth and exercise your authority, because the days ahead are yours.
The victories of tomorrow are your responsibility.
Use your voice to let times know that there is NO time for a lack of purpose.
How do I love thee?
Let me count the ways...
First, be motivated by the possibility that your lives will serve a higher purpose.
Second, you must close the gap between "I have a dream" and a dream fulfilled.
Lastly, as our daily thoughts and opportunities all lead to you, I hope you strive towards *overachievement* and *perfectionism*
and endless boundaries,...
as all this provides great insight.

The Fight of One Black Man

This fight I am in
or have been having
does not have rounds
or a referee.
It's just me against the world.
I am not saying it's about Black
or White.
It's about what is right
and what is wrong.
Right now I feel as if I am in the boxing ring of a heavy weight fight
and it is the tenth round,
halfway through a 20 round bout.
I am half full
and half empty;
either way I can not give up.
I trained too hard for this fight
and I have too much to lose
if I give up,
quit or
even just ease up.
So, I guess I'll be like Muhammad Ali-
"Float like a butterfly and sting like a bee.
Because this is one Black man, you shall not beat."
I don't need Gatorade to drink
nor do I need rest.
All I really need is FAITH AND BELIEF IN GOD,
then LOVE AND CONFIDENCE IN MYSELF.
With all these things I will conquer and win the hardest fight of my life.

Feelings and Emotions

Sometimes I laugh; other times I cry. I often drift into a daze, staring deeply up in the sky. I find myself at ease- studying Mother Nature from my observance. I speculate; it's a type of peace maker. Put here with its own uniqueness as a sign from the creator. Sometimes I compare my pain with wild flowers that die from lack of rain or lack of sunshine.

Could it be their pain is greater than mine? Is it true that love is blind? But could that change through the course of time? As an actor, my character goes through the scenarios. My feelings get uncontrollable.

Dealing with something so emotional, such as life, but it is what you make it. As humans, we fall into trends, but as a nation, the cycle we must break it. So many debatable issues.

So much pain when your family misses you. So much rage when the cops frisk you. My people done shed tears for years, letting their feelings and emotions, soak into tissue. I cry not physically, but mentally on the inside. I deal with my dilemma's consequences.

Not dealing with any pride. We must stand for something, or get knocked off balance over nothing.

Obstacles don't get destroyed. Unless it's our hands doing the crushing, we need to slow down.

Stop rushing; think about precautions. You could lose me; I could lose you.

The world will continue. The sky will still be blue. Do we share the same goals or have plans to meet in the abode? Best believe, feelings and emotions change as the body grows old.

Feelings and emotions.

Most High

First of all, this is not about getting high
or being high from drugs or alcohol.
Ok- it is about being high from the Most High.
I know of the Most High
but I really want to get to know the Most High.
He has taken me away from the chemical high
and is still taking away things in my life
that I don't need, want or desire.
I don't have to explain all the details
but I was in the streets
and in different sheets
with too many freaks.
I thank the Most High that I did not have to go see the doctor
or get chased by baby daddies.
The Most High has blessed me with so many things in life;
I don't think I can write all of these things down on paper.
But the few things I can list are
my life,
my job,
my roof,
food and clothes on my back,
healthy children,
mom and dad,
a chance to start life over drug free,
free from stress,
no cell or cell mate,
the ability to read and write,
a chance to go back to school
and get my culinary degree;
one of my talents is to cook.

Most of all, the ability to stand
and be a REAL MAN
for THE MOST HIGH.
Be Blessed.

Shawqui Y. Novoa

I Vow Not

I vow not to deteriorate the street corner.
Not to take a post or night shift watch,
on our corner, or to use my eye for the look out.
I vow not to help supply the drugs in our
neighborhood where I live
or where my forefathers had once been slaves
and sweat for me to grow.
I vow not disrespect the woman
who worked hard to build a future for her offspring;
who stood on that cold corner late at night
just to catch the bus for a long ride to work;
who slept until her stop was next.
The one who worked two jobs
so food was on our plates,
and worked hard to get home before it was late.
The one who never took a vacation
out of the hood.
The one whose life was within me.
The one I wore the dress she sweated for.

I vow not.

Jai Braden

One Body One Mind

Butterflies in your stomach
an eye for an eye
a smart mouth
a toothless grin
on the nose
lead foot
Not by the hairs on my chinny chin chin
the upper hand
a trick knee
a green thumb
ring finger
a broken heart
a fat ass
blue balls
a wooden leg
nappy hair
Complete silence
chaos
revelation
Armageddon
holocaust
redemption
calm
riot
flames
waves
faith
insanity
submission
infinity

control
electricity
pain
joy
laws
love
war
peace
one life
one death
One Body
One Mind

Darren Reed

The Drum

Through chaotic melodies
you exist, repeating
yourself in syncopated
thumps, cool and consistent,
changing tempo, gyrating bodies,
guiding souls to freedom.
You came with us when we came
and we honor you in cars and clubs,
rattling metal fixtures,
beating life into us steady
and strong,
guiding our
path to
freedom.

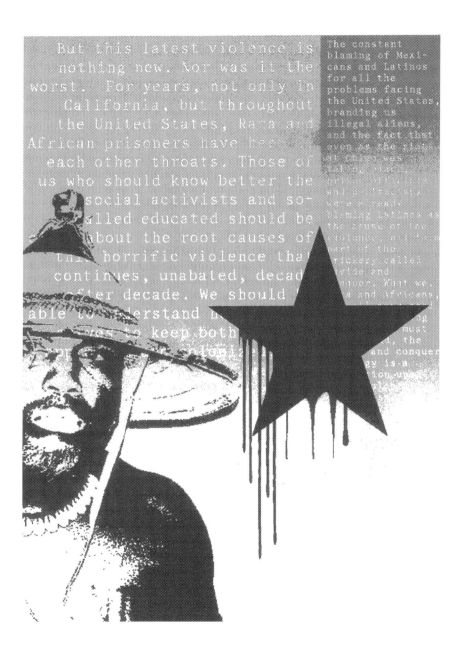

But this latest violence is nothing new. Nor was it the worst. For years, not only in California, but throughout the United States, Raza and African prisoners have been [at] each other throats. Those of us who should know better the social activists and so-called educated should be [clear] about the root causes of this horrific violence that continues, unabated, decade after decade. We should [be] able to understand h[ow]... to keep both...

The constant blaming of Mexicans and Latinos for all the problems facing the United States, branding us illegal aliens, and the fact that even as the riots...

Shawqui Y. Novoa

Divided Seed

Condemned.
Divided seed,
even as an embryo.
She was raised under harsh conditions,
and subjected even as a child.
It's not about black or white.
While she thus maintained
utter personal indifference.
Acquainted herself
after battling racism;
a person of color,
one psychological study.
Overcame racism and rose to the top,
only to a hostile world
from a Latina without having
to deal with someone from
her own race.
Who am I
African-Latina-American
emotional and physical I am.
I am an embryo from a dividing seed,
who should have been treated more
carefully.
I wasn't white enough,
the pigmentation of my skin.
I wasn't black enough.
Who am I
I'm just a embryo from a dividing seed.
My hair isn't straight enough,
My skin isn't white enough.

But yet, my smile
my laugh
my cry, my tears.
It's all the same.
We are God's embryo before we are divided.
Carefully.

I Wanna Be

I wanna be an old black woman with wrinkles & heartaches & lies…
I wanna be an old black woman 'cause only the strongest survive.
I wanna be an old black woman; sometimes cynical, sarcastic, & gay…
I wanna be an old black woman 'cause Rome wasn't built in a day.

I wanna remember when life was good & real music helped to free your
soul…
When livin' was hard & dyin' was free & a black man made me whole.

I wanna be an old black woman 'cause her womb was the cradle for life…
I wanna be an old black woman 'cause her wit is as sharp as a knife.
I wanna be an old black woman; her nails no longer manicured,
I wanna be an old black woman who's lived long enough to have her soul
pure.

For God has governed her presence from the very beginning of time…
He has held her head when heavy & mentally massaged her mind.
He taught her the TRUE meaning of unconditional love…
and given direction & guidance using the Father, the Son, & the Dove.

So the next time you spot an old black woman, take time to step out of her
way…
'cause that woman may very well be me; I pray I make it there one day.

Basil Mustafa

A King Upon A Throne

Upon my throne made of gold, silver and brass ...
Is hieroglyphic writing expressing my presence upon the planet?
Looking over my Kingdom, God has bestowed me with
true responsibility among my people and my own actions.
With great power comes great responsibility.
One rule is to keep it real with myself, others, and my Lord.
Women come by the dozen wanting to be my Queen or love slave.
As the King and a ruler, of my domain, I must be careful of temptations as a
man of God.
As a man I've fallen to the pleasures of life's lust- making repentance a ritual.
True prayer makes a true King; that I know.
My staff and words of power are monitored by mortal gossip.
Some say that the King is an ultra man; some say a cosmonaut from the
stars.
But the flesh always brings me back to mortality.
My science is like treasure.
I must safeguard it at all times.
There is a duty of the King, know this.
Everything is not easy and the Queen must be protected at all times;
sometimes even from the King, if he's not focused.
Upon my throne made of gold, silver and brass, being a King is
responsibility.
So, you have to do the best you can in the name of God.
For my rug of meditation made of silk, satin, and cotton is a gift from
Heaven.
I give great respect to the master of the universal whole.
Upon my throne made of gold, silver, and brass you must have knowledge to
be a King.

O Mothership Come (Ezekiel 1:4-28)

In giving US the light, so gracious was HE
to take the life-giving Sun and split it into threes;
one part for the gods,
a part for the earths,
and the rest for the seven seas ...

Our Holy Architect and His sacred Star Children
laid the foundations for the pyramids just for US to start building
in accordance to His guidance and planning.
Although WE lack knowledge, wisdom, and understanding
that WE all travel on the same
360 degree plane
fashioned after the u-n-I-verse;
WE, the lesser gods and earths.
A u-n-I-verse that moves in line with US;
one nation under a groove in time with US;
as WE proceed and move on ....

But the other men studied the occult
to find an *elixir to life*.
Yea, right-
Sounded more like *eugenics*.
Children of the u-n-I-verse, don't you get it?!?
Whether a rare evolutionary find
or the product of intelligent design,
WE got an arch enemy
who practiced alchemy
as the fore runner of the sciences.
And according to the prophecies of Nostradamus,
by the year 2012,

nothing will differ the Earth from Hell.
But swing down, as sweet chariot
comes forth to carry US
back home in a while
accompanied by the Messianic Star Child.
Because my People got this Mothership Connection
that ain't even being talked about in our history lessons.

THREE

WE must also change by seeking Black love and finding our soul connections…

In the Beginning

When God made Adam, He waited until after the night had been separated from the day, the water from the land, and each space was populated with living things. Then, forming him from the dust and breathing life into his being, God gave Adam dominion over all that was. As Adam roamed the land eating freely of the plants for food and naming each as he went, God decided to supply Adam a helper.

"The Lord God said it is not good for man to be alone. I will make a helper suitable for him." (Genesis 2:18)

With this declaration God created all the beasts of the land and birds of the air, bringing each to Adam to see what he would name them. As Adam named the animals and cared for the land, he did not recognize a helper suitable for him. He noticed the bird with its like and the beast of the land as well but for his own kind he recognized no alignment.

God rejoiced at Adams reckoning, for you see He needed Adam to freely understand *his* own need. God needed Adam to know within himself neither beast, fowl nor green life can replace the help only one like you can supply. God knew before the beginning of time the worlds need for woman, but He allowed Adam time to realize his heart's desire on his own. With Adam's awakening, God took him into a deep sleep.

"While he was sleeping He took one of the man's ribs and closed up the place with flesh. Then the Lord God made a woman from the rib he had taken out of the man and He brought her to the man." (Genesis 2: 21-22)

God Almighty, creator of all things, could have easily created Eve from the same dust He used to form Adam, but He chose instead to create her from man. From the bone that covered mans heart he formed woman. Woman means *womb of man* and from the beginning of creation by God's design man was meant to protect the heart of woman and she to protect the mind of man.

Fast forward. It is now obviously and painfully clear to see that something has gone wrong. Women are playing the role of men and convincing themselves that they don't need a man to be whole or to be stable or even to be a parent. Men are laying down with men and standing on marriage alters with other men and fighting for their right to do so while the rest, in such scarcity, are using, abusing, and running so much game that no one can see clearly where to even begin to heal or mend the brokenness. And it is all broken.

In the beginning, God intended black love between a man and woman to be free, pure, true, fruitful and lasting. But it is broken. The backbone of love has been broken in the cavities of slave ships. Stripped and sold on the auction block and hung strangely from trees to shrivel up and die. To be blown away by the wind. Black love was institutionalized by Jim Crow laws that belittled and dehumanized the black man so that the womb of man-protector of his mind-no longer desires to fulfill her God ordained duty.

She despises him for what he lacks. A lacking that he was set up and designed to experience by a racist system hoping he would never get back to realizing and remembering the greatness God planned for him in the beginning. He despises her for her strength. Because of her pretending to be the man, he leaves her to protect her own heart. Caring not about the lies, distrust, or chaos that he leaves behind.

It was never meant to be like this! This is not the way we can survive. Women, we need our men! We must build them up and fill them up with the word of God. We must praise them and soothe their tired, frustrated minds with cooling balm so they can sustain the brutal attacks of racism that they receive daily within tasks as seemingly mundane as driving to work. We need our men to be our lovers, friends, providers, fathers to our children, cradles of our souls, and protectors of our hearts.

Men you need us. Not a babies' mama or some trim on the side. You need Eve. We- black women, designed for love in the beginning- are your Eve. The original wife God formed especially for you, of you, to be with you- working and growing together forever. Stop pretending that when you see us you don't recognize your mothers, daughters, and sisters in our eyes and in our tears. Protect our hearts men; we need you too- even if we're too proud to say so. Wrap us in your strong, world-building arms and melt our pride. Crack down the walls we've built to protect our own hearts and love us! Rejoice in our thick, full lips and hips made wide from birthing a nation. Rub your fingers through our hair and make us know it will be alright because you say so.

We must get back to the beginning so that we can move forward to the future in love together. No longer afraid or unsure, but trusting and believing enough in God's original plan to take a chance on each other.

Nicole Williams

His Kiss

His kiss altered remaining
days of my existence.
Language of ancestors
slipped through full lips.
Intelligence of Langston,
power of Malcolm.
His words speak of
present events,
but his spirit suggests
chrome shackles,
cotton fields and
freedom rides.
Sit-ins at white-only counters,
sipping water from
colored-only fountains.
Short steps to the back of the
bus until the boycott.
Tired feet,
tired of waiting
at bus stops.
Old soul like he built arches
and parted the Red Sea.
He opened his eyes and
I became his Queen.
No longer would he allow legal
mind rapes at midnight,
colorless hands divided
emancipated legs;
my only symbol of freedom.
Entered inside and

stole the one thing
I thought I could keep
since my skin they despised,
Sadly, it too was stolen.
Until his kiss gave me
access into a world of our own.
A world where us two were free.
Free at last, free at last
Thank God almighty we are
free at last,
and we can grow together.
Live in love where colored-only
fountains never existed.
Bus boycotts were because bus
fare was too expensive.
Chrome shackles were a fashion mistake,
sitting at the back of the
bus was by choice, and
white-only counters are a
color of marble tops.
Freedom rides were about
personal revival and
mind rapes were about
momentary failure.
Through his kiss I sensed,
through his eyes I saw,
black was never the color of
oppression,
but the color of night.

Taya R. Baker

I Know Black Love ...

Will I know it when I see it
will I recognize its kisses
or
will it call me by name

Will it whisper in my ear
or
will I perhaps feel the same

Will warm breezes first caress my face
or
will it surprise me and seemingly defy time and space

Will I heave and gasp for breath
will I stand shoulders back, erect
or
perhaps there will be sound effects

Will I know it when I see it
Will I taste it
Will I touch it
Will I feel it
Maybe hear it

Will it make me cry or laugh (or maybe pass a little gas)
will I smile uncontrollably
will it fall down to one knee and ask to marry me

I'm sure I'll remember the day, the night, the hour
love took me under its power

I'll smile, I'll laugh, I'll cry
I'll probably wink an eye

Because love will have found me

I'll know it when I see it
I'll recognize its kisses
I'll know it when I feel it
I'll call it by its name…
Black love

Perhaps

As Jacuzzi bubbles rise
and fade away like troubles,
we share nights filled full
of ambient candle light
and a warm fire place.
You can't hide the desire on your face
as we hear Roy Ayers
and we smell the aromas of incense
and candle scents in the air.
I want you.
I want you.
I have to have you.
I grab you.
Caught up in the splendor
of this sweet surrender makes me yours
and it makes you mine
perhaps for a lifetime.
Our climaxes building
from overlapping sounds of Maxwell and Cassandra Wilson.
Not knowing where the night went
leaves our mornings to be spent
with Marvin Gaye and Minnie Riperton.
Laughing together.
Together.
Listening
to that dawn's early light glistening.
Completing each other's thoughts.
Both of us caught
because I, too, miss our bodies being entangled.
Hanging onto

our last words.
Baby,
maybe you have heard
that while life also happens,
we got our own thing
which promises to bring
celebrations,
champagne bubbles,
and libations chasing away troubles
and washing away burdens.
Said what you wanted and deserved it;
a man of your own.
A growing man; not necessarily a man who is grown.
Perhaps I am him.

He Abandoned Me

I loved him
with everything in me
I loved him
I met him and I knew
that he would forever change my life
and he did
with the sweetest words
he rewrote my love realities
feeding me gentle kisses
and opening my soul
with his musings of we
He convinced me to
let down my guard
trust him like no other
he freed me from the bonds of
fear
hesitancy
and uncertainty
then that mutherfucka ...
turned on me
even as he sang sweet songs to me
he was betraying our reality
with his singular pursuits
he destroyed my happiness
left me confused and unbalanced
all because he could no longer see
the viability of we
and I hate him
with every fiber of my soul
I hate him

the way he said my name
like no other
the way he fed me lies
like they were sweet pecan pies
the way he wrapped my heart
around his every single finger
only to leave me laying on the floor
heart broken
spirit bruised
soul in pieces
because he was really only a facsimile
of the love he pretended to offer me
and I hate him
with every fiber in my soul
I hate him
the way he used my weakness
to undermine me
used my secret desires
to unwind me
the way he used love
to seduce me into his web
only to abandon me
to empty memories tied to
soul searching uncertainties
as I struggle to create a new reality
outside of the one love seduced me into
and that bitch shattered so selfishly
and I hate him
with every fiber in my soul
I hate him
lovingly

Shawqui Y. Novoa

You Ain't Right Brother

You ain't right brother.

You're full of bull.

You ain't right brother,

with me your cup was full.

You ain't right brother.

If I was a man,

I'd want to hurt you.

You ain't right brother.

But you can't break my will.

You've tried to steal my soul.

Stripped me naked.

Down to the bone.

I was better off being alone.

You ain't right brother.

I can't understand your mentality.

I was your relief.

I was your freedom key.

   You were silently scamming to get out.

But once you were out,

you chose to put a lock on me.

No respect, no respect.

You ain't right brother.

Want Him to Want to (part III)

I want to be
equally yoked.
And wherever it's broke
I want healing to overflow.
I want to know
that we
are in the same boat.
Sink or float.
Only God knows
where the road
ahead will lead.
I want our strength to be
found in the union of we.
I want every note
to be in accord.
And be sure
that when I
lay it all on the line
I won't have to be afraid
this time.
I don't want him
to make up
for every break up
that scarred me in the past.
And I don't want to pay for
the last
woman who turned out not to be
what she claimed that she
was initially.
I want to believe

that we are exactly
where we are supposed to be.

I want to be
easy in his company.
Want him to be
trouble-free
in mine.
If it's peace that he's
trying to find
I want to create
that state
of calm
into which he reclines.
My arms stretch wide
and I've got plenty of room
if he wants to
come inside.
I want him to say
that he's ready
to begin his forever
today.
And I will plant my feet
in the promise of this sweet
ever-after.
I can breathe without him
but I'd rather
not.
I want him to know my every spot.
And I want to submit to
what I cannot stop.
I want him to admit to
knowing what he's got.

I want him
not to be intimidated
by what I bring to the table.
I don't want to
do this alone
but I am able.
I want his bond

to be his word.
I want to hear him
and feel like I've been heard.
Don't want to be deterred
by cold feet
or loss of nerve.
I want his best
because that's what I give
and that's what I deserve.
I want everything to be
exactly as it appears.
Don't want to have to guess
if what he confesses
is sincere.
And I want it to be clear
beyond every doubt
and every fear
so that I can completely adhere.
I want him to be convinced.
Totally confident
that I'm cool right here

I want him to catch
every tear that I cry
even if he doesn't understand
the what, the who, the why.
I want him to have the insight
to recognize
that words can be taken adversely
and be man enough to apologize
when it's his words
that hurt me.
Won't always have the answer for every adversity.
Still we talk until we
collectively arrive
at compromise.
And we pray
before we lay
our love down each night
that joy comes in the morning
and resolution is realized

with the dawning.
We don't always have to see
eye to eye
as long as we
stay focused on the prize.
I want to achieve
the highest highs
with him.
Fly with him.
Exceed the limits
of the sky with him.

I want to
grow old with him.
Still holding him
down
in our golden years.
Time is no test.
From the moment we say yes,
I want to persevere.
Find our way clear
of the obstacles that threaten to interfere.
I want to be able
to look back
and feel that
every leg of the trip
was absolutely worth it.
Not that it's going to be perfect;
nothing ever is.
But we can respect that.
So our objective
is not perfection
no matter the direction
we find ourselves stepping.
I want to eternally
celebrate the blessing
of our connection.

Haven't you ever heard before
that when it's real it endures?
So we never lose sight of the vision.

Embracing our positions.
That's what keeps us strong.
Even when tempted we never roam.
And we're not delusional.
Temptation will always come.
But thank God we're both grown
and our commitment to this
is always number one.
I want him to know
that he has someone at home
who loves him.
Even when it's hard to
we find a way to get through.
That's what our allegiance
guides us to do.
So that we can remain
stable with the
groundwork that we've laid.
And even in his absence
my heart will grow fonder.
My vow will never falter.
My eyes will never wander.
Let no man
or woman
put asunder
what God has placed
His foundation up under.
So glad that I can finally
cease from just wanting this to be.
You see
He is the he
that I prayed for
And what God had in store
was worth the wait
and so much more.

Taya R. Baker

NIGGAH Please

NIGGAHS be rollin'
NIGGAHS be strollin'
schemin'
devisin'
mishandlin' the TRUTH
lookin' for the next big BREAK
   - - maybe takin' what they can TAKE
leavin' devastation and destruction in their WAKE
Get a job…NIGGAH
Get an education…NIGGAH
Get some self-respect…NIGGAH
NIGGAH…pull up your pants
…enunciate a word…or two
Call me by my name (I ain't your Boo),
so I can once again
be proud to love you
…Negro…African American…young Black man

Staci Celeste

Black Man

There is nothing like a black man.
Your rhythm, your strut, the curve of your butt
all make me smile.
Even through tears, I've smiled at the phenomenon of you.
From Wall Street to behind the wall you are
beautifully hued, fighting to stay true,
pimping, jiving, nine-to-fiving,
lovely regal,
royal king you are.
Rise above the whip scars and hear.
Hear God's voice and understand that you are the original man.
Jesus' twin.
Black man there is nothing like you.
No sunrise can out bright you.
No lion can outfight you.
You are smooth- especially when you're rough.
You excel- especially when it's tough.
You're a black man.
They marvel at your resilience
while attempting to sabotage your brilliance.
But on your feet each time you land, like a mountain you stand.
Beautiful, black, chocolate brother there is truly no other like you.
Stimulating, intense, passionate lover of mine take my hand.
Let's seek to understand this journey together.

Shawqui Y. Novoa

Drumbeat

As I lay and hear the sounds of the drum,
my heart flutters with palpitations.
I want to dance for you.
I want to sing a song with my body up and down.
Can't you see me with your heart?
Can you feel my thoughts caress me?
With your hands gluing from my head to my toe,
smell me- smell me with your tongue.
Taste me with your mind
Feel me with your thoughts
Free me like the drumbeat.
Fill me with your emptiness.
Hear the drums.
Hear the drums.

Darren Reed

Honduran Summer

Caribbean breezes stroll gently
along her face, hugging
the contours of her beauty.
White sands mold her,
leaving imprints of hearts turned
upside down along the shore.
Echoes of my thoughts beckon to her
but she doesn't hear.
Through squinting eyes I peer,
watching the sun kiss apricot hues
across her body, matching
her with the glowing sunset.
I followed her to this paradise
where she and its purity are one.
I snap mental pictures
hoping to still-frame her essence
but it is too free to capture.
Inhaling the summertime air,
pleasures consumes me.
I asked her to marry me today,
she said yes.

Letter to the Black Woman:

Loving You (part V)

Let us explore, explore into depths of the cells, the center thinking, the mastering of thought, the lust of learning before indulging. Practicing actions before words, there's nothing greater than making love with the mind.

O, the grinding focus of ones' path to paradise to become one. Let us make love to the center thing before the soul, 'cause the mind is a terrible thing to waste.

Mind before pleasure, a divine ritual of love, the true essence of love. Understanding that the body is a temple, a place of worship clean from sin.

Through the mind I see the inside of your temple, sacred with peace. So many chambers of love within it. It is expressed with silver and gold, so magnificent it displays the artifacts of God bringing you to my heart.

I fell in love witnessing God's grace and creativity all around you. On the walls I see the math of birth and how you deliver through the wombs of science. I realize nothing can destroy it; only you.

Please take care of it, so, I can visit again.

FOUR

And WE must reclaim our children- all of them ...

Nicole Williams

Injustice or Just Us:

Planting Seeds to Grow a Stronger Youth

"I see children, no longer innocent; their minds have been conditioned by media's unrealistic expectations of beauty and self image. They run amid drug transactions, dodging bullets for exercise and play hide-go-seek with the police. They are no longer children, they are no more." I quote this from a poem of mine entitled 'Over the Rhine, 2002'.

Are we failing the youth? Have we done everything in our power to instill in them morals, beliefs, and character for them to grow and become respectful and productive citizens? As I write the introduction to this chapter of poetry I find myself struggling to find the right words on how important it is that my generation do all it can to take back our youth. I struggle because I write this as a parent of an 8-year old boy whom I want to grow up in a world where life is the most precious gift there is. A world where it is cool to be smart and our children value their educations more than the latest pair of Jordans or the newest model of the *i*-phone. I write as an educator, as a poet, and as a concerned citizen. I write as a human being who questions: are 'We' doing enough to make the children of today understand the importance of life and education?

Is it any surprise that the youth of today value things that depreciate and glorify celebrities who publicize how they made millions without a college education? Should I be shocked when I hear first graders say they want to be rappers instead of radio executives or football players instead of owning the team? Our youth are constantly bombarded with images of 11 year old girls who look 21, appearing on the cover of magazines in little or no clothing. We live in a society where 17 year old boys talk explicitly about sexual acts behind tight beats and our children dance with no clue to the meaning behind the lyrics. No, it no longer surprises me when children are not more imaginative in their replies.

Reality television makes our children feel inferior because their sweet 16 is a modest birthday party with several friends, cake, ice cream, and affordable gifts. Instead, our children see sweet 16s that are aired on MTV, costing more than the average home and including lavish gifts such as Range Rovers along with a personal celebrity concert. It is no wonder our children don't appreciate the little things we can offer them in life, such as a quality education, family time, or a quiet holiday dinner with family and friends. And while our children's lives may not be being aired on television, they are emulating what they see.

We are failing our youth by not speaking up about what our children are viewing on television and hearing on the radio. We are failing our youth by not providing more positive examples in our homes, our communities, and our schools. We must turn off the radio, turn off the television and allow our children to tune into our reality. If we don't, our children will continue to believe that education is of no importance and that life is not a precious gift. We must reclaim the youth; get them off the street and back into our homes and the classroom. As parents we must remember that we are our child's first teacher and our homes- their first classroom. We must plant, nurture, and water seeds that will grow a stronger youth.

Mama … I Tried

Mama I did what you said … trying to bring the family back together. I've been chasing my brothers and sisters through all types of weather. Baby boy ain't even listening to me- just telling me "**whatever!**" Baby girl mad at somebody named Tyrone but takes it out on her babies' daddy Trevor. I saw Big Sis. I went to her askin' where she been? But she ran into an **abandoned house,** Mama. And didn't invite me in. I saw Big Bro … the one we used to call "**Man**". He just jumped the fence with your 21 inch in hand. He said you'd understand. He'd bring it back after the game went off. Mama, I saw **daddy**. I tried to tell him the lights & gas was off. But he was with some lady and kept talking to me like I was lost. Then he told me not to get too close to him because of how much his new Jordans cost! I did what you said Mama; I said "**Say Cheese daddy.**" But he got mad and walked away from me because that lady's little girl had to pee.
Don't **cry**, Mama, don't cry! You did all that you could do Mama. Don't cry.

I'm gone do right by you, Mama. If I'm the only thing **going right** for you, Mama. Don't cry, Mama, don't cry … I'll try again tomorrow …
I'm sorry **Mama … I tried** …

Our Fathers

WE lost legacies
as our fathers failed
at fatherhood
and then fell farther
from the 'hood
through the paternal lineage
and the patronage
of the pimpin' papi
making babies
with a baby mama
while making drama
out of daddy's maybes,
mama's babies,
and more legacies lost.
Descendant of this,
our daddies WE missed
and WE continue to pay the costs.

2nd *Generation Son*

I am a second generation son
American bred and born
carrying blood
from other nations
separated
long before my time
so, instead I embrace
and carry proudly
what you outwardly see
-this African skin.

My daughter is born
to the son of a son
of a son of the island.
So I endeavor
never to allow
that bit of Hispanic within me now
to be lost or ignored
no more
than I have allowed her to ignore also being African.
Although English is the only language I know,
how else will she know
from what little is shown
to African American children?
I speak broken Spanish
and few African words
except for the Swahili I have heard.
But if I do not show her
she may see
and she will not understand.

Then what kind of father
or man
would I be?
Pieces of me
have already been forgotten
before they were taught to me.
I am trying to retain
whatever remains
from the heritage within my name
and the blood coursing through my veins.
The blood of conquistadors and ocean explorers
and Zulu Kings and Ashanti warriors
and Alabama back roads
and Cleveland, Ohio
and Philadelphia streets
is all within the blood both our hearts beat.
And she needs to know this.

Desmond Storm E Jones

Hung Up

While wearing the clothes of a fatherless child …

I've sat in the window
    waiting for my daddy to come and make
    me smile.
All the while
Mama cussin' you
Phone rings:
Your no good _____ _____
wants to talk to you.
Come get the phone.
Hello? When you comin'?
But you promised **this week**.
Mama said: You can't pay child support
    you don't need to see me.
She standing right here & said
she don't want to talk to you.

Daddy, what you gonna do?
Who can I run to?
Should I run like you do?
    From anything and everything
    you can't lie to, conquer, or screw.
Physical absence is your disguise.
    Mama still trippin' off your lies.
I'm unsupervised
    listening to Mama's growing hate
    the sequel to my demise
    and the family.

I hope I don't grow up to be like …
Hello?
Hello?
He Hung Up!

Black Children

WE are the pain,
the shame,
and the burden
that lasts a lifetime from a childhood of hurting.

WE are the bi-product of four or five fatherless generations.

The world's greatest industrialized nation
has left herself a legacy of collateral damage
in single Black mothers finding some way to manage
day to day finances.
Heading households,
dodging dicks,
and providing for welfare and health
while failing to generate generational wealth.

That, too, becomes collateralized
as the damages go so much farther
than just being Black Children without fathers.

Many people celebrated Obama's inauguration as a great step in the realization of "Martin Luther King, Jr.'s dream." Many of those who oppose the oppression of Black people, deep in their heart and their guts, see his presidency as paving the way to the day when Black people can fully participate in society as equals. Some say the election is a big step in changing the hearts and minds of white people so that they will see Black people *as people*, as *human beings*. Others, meanwhile, go so far as to claim that the election *proves* that America now only judges people not "by the color of their skin but by the content of their character" (to quote King's "I Have a Dream" speech)...and that any more talk about oppression is "just an excuse."

And all those celebrating—including, of course, Obama himself—claim this shows the superiority of the American Constitution. King himself cast his dream as a dream that America "live out the true meaning of its creed" as spelled out in the Constitution and Declaration of Independence.

So, *does* Obama's election signal a major step toward realizing Martin Luther King, Jr.'s dream? We're going to analyze that. And to really get into that, we are going to have to raise a further question: is the dream that King laid out 45 years ago one that can lead to emancipation? Or is it in fact a snare, or worse—one that people should reject, and take up something different?

The American Nightmare

First, let's get into the circ[...] that led into the Civil Righ[...] and [...] Liber[...] No[...] the [...]

of hundreds of people. They were determined to be free, to "not be turned around." This came at a time of great international challenges to the U.S. system and of major economic changes, especially in the South; and as a result of all that coming together, basic rights were won.

Black people now have the right to vote. It is no longer illegal for Black people to go to the same schools as whites. In all parts of the country, some employment and educational opportunities opened up, and some Black people obtained better paying factory jobs and entered colleges in much greater numbers. Today, there are more Black professionals, educators, scientists and academics than ever before, and the number of Black elected officials has grown dramatically. And Barack Obama has been sworn in as President.

In other words, the system was forced to allow a section of Black people to "move on up." This is what people point to when people say [...] Ob[...] the realization of the [...] little closer.

Siyahamba

Siyahamb' ekukhanyen' kwenkhos',
Siyahamb' ekukhanyen' kwenkhos' …

What joy it brings
to hear my daughter sing, "we are walking in the light of GOD."
Standing in full sight of GOD
and remaining right despite the odds
of mastering the trials and errors of doing what a father does.
Abu means *father of.*
Full-fledged fatherhood with no want nor means of reversal.
Playing the part of a father means its with no rehearsal.
But my GOD is eternal;
His truth is universal.
So, I never walk alone.

Siyahamba, hamba,
Siyahamba, hamba,
Ooh- Siyahamb' ekukhanyen' kwenkhos'.

Michael J. Crump

548

548 is a number that's on a bird's wings.
548 is a song that the fat lady sings.

548 is a baseball that is hit out to the right.
Writing shit like this is why I don't sleep at night.
I keep saying these numbers like I forgot to play the lottery.
But I have already lost the game; was it pick 4? No. Only pick 3.
548! 548! I keep yelling with every breath from my lungs.
Screaming like this sometimes feels like a bullet from that 9mm gun.
People have said take it as a blessing- it could be good luck.
But when I see those numbers, the wheels are spinning but I am stuck.
It's a great opportunity, these are the sounds I hear all day.
I glare at them hard and then shout it's 548- not 25 ok?
548 is the distance in miles between she, he, he, and he.
I'm not happy with the one but I will truly miss the times 3.
Will I be standing there as they get in the car and say goodbye?
NO because this is what hurt is and I'm so tired of crying.
So don't mention 548 to me if you call me wanting to play
'cause I'll be sitting at home without them on every freaking Saturday.

Goodbye for now.

Darren Reed

Empty Rocker

She rocked bundled kids
to school each morning
sipping from a plastic
cup filled with love.
The number of her rocks are
in the thousands,
rocking generations on.

She was the neighborhood watch,
commanding respect with each rock,
offering warm hugs *and*
switch whippings.

She met dawn in the rocker
and rocked the stars to our block
at night. A baby sitter
to my mom *and* me, an institution.

Her rocker is empty now
and nearby kids run wild.
My children won't know the joy
and comfort of her rocking,
my stories will have to do.

Can I Please See My Kids?

I apologize for my past true lies.
I didn't know then the after effects would
materialize
like this!
Restraining order got my back against the fence.
I can't defend myself while I watch you
teach my kids against me. Can I please see my kids?

It was lovely when **you** loved me.
When you just **loved me**.
I can't change how or why you **hate**
when I know that displaced hate is how the kids
relate
to an existence that had **everything** to do
with what **we** did.
I know I came by at a **bad** time
like the **last** time or the **next** time, but Can I please see my kids???

Just because I don't have keys
doesn't mean we've got to be enemies.
And that bullshit from child support's
pulpit
will never amount to what it really means
to **spend time** with their Daddy.
Not that 20 minute, supervised, front hallway visitation
while you **cussing** at me
or teaching them how to interact with me. Can I please see my kids …

I know you know I wear the clothes of a
Fatherless Child

I've **waited** the "**Wait**"
I've **cried** that "**Cry**"
Wondering if I was **the reason why**
there was nobody called:
"**Daddy**"
in my life
Or Mama's home, leaving me with stories of
"**Yo no good daddy!**"
to size myself up to when I got to be grown.
I know I called at a **bad** time
like the **last** time or the **next** time, but
could you at least put my kids on
the phone? Can I please see my kids …

I don't plan to teach the kids against you
but we can't even see **eye to I**.
How can I encourage them to **abide** by you
when they can't **see** me?
Or should I wait for you to call me
when they take their **first steps** …
toward **penitentiary**?
Or found on the doorsteps of a **drug dependency**?
Or last seen in these **streets** looking for the **love** they
should be getting from **You and Me**?
So before you call the police on me,
Can I please see **our** kids so
I can encourage them to be <u>better than me</u>**?!**

WE Speak (2 Save the Babies)

Most were born in the early 90s or late 80s
so they are still babies.
But what is going on
is that somewhere WE went wrong
with the laws or with their enforcement
by merely matching force with
our lack of teaching them morality
leading to incarceration, mortality,
and violence
as WE balance our right to remain silent
with our freedom of speech.
But then fail at practicing what WE preach.

Nicole Williams

She Spoke

I was on the 17 heading downtown.
On the bus was a woman
who defined dignity.
She sat solemnly with her legs crossed
and deep rooted look on her face.
We talked and exchanged
polite conversation.
She said she was sad because
she knew what I was facing.
Told me it was hard but to always
keep my faith in God.
She said hell only lasts sometime
but heaven, heaven lasts forever.
Told me to wait out the storm cause
it's going to rain,
but you can't stop the sun from shining.
And she spoke 'bout how she swam
cross seas with shackles on feet and
bruises on her back so deep
that she could feel them in her soul.
She spoke about civil rights,
strong black men,
how to uplift our race and education.
She said my generation lacks these things.
Told me that black men need
to stop looking at young women as just
ass and tits and stop wondering
about the prize between the thighs and
start thinking about life and how that
young woman creates life.

And she spoke,
"Women are the closest thing to
God and men should have high
regard for that!"
She spoke,
"but if a woman don't have
respect for herself,
how can she demand respect?"
She spoke, about
love and marriage and told me
how she was married fifty years yesterday
but last year her husband suffered
from a stroke, he was living on life support
and what a cherished life and
how she cherishes life.
She spoke about our ancestors who
paved the way.
All the righteous teachers,
some I'd never heard of.
She said that's because you
learn black history in school.
Told me to educate myself.
She spoke,
"The truth ain't in those textbooks
you read, college girl.
Look in my eyes; you can see your history,
his history, our history.
These politicians don't speak the truth.
This country was built on lies."
She spoke about our people
fighting on the front line and dying
behind deceit.
She spoke
"We haven't won our battle
with this country.
We fought for truth and they told us lies.
We believed and kept on
living barely breathing.
Just 'cause we drive expensive cars
and have titles at our jobs don't mean
the battle has been won.

If terrorists hadn't attacked
America, home of the brave
we'd be the enemy behind the gates
"trapped."
She spoke the truth,
but got off that bus still with
the deep rooted look on her face.
She spoke with dignity.
She spoke with grace.
She spoke to me.

Master, How Am I Doin?

Breakin' news!
The slaves have been set free!
News in the future- they're too free!
"Man I just got a house with a picket fence and a dog."
Master, how am I doin?
On the plantation were picket fences and hunting dogs to search for runaway slaves.
"Man I'll never stop eatin' pork"
Master, how am I doin?
They gave hog slop to the slaves to be spiteful.
"Happy Thanksgiving, I love it!"
Master, how am I doin?
The Indians taught the whites how to eat to live in return they kill them.
"I put my Christmas tree up and got me a Santa Claus."
Master, how am I doin?
Even though Jeremiah 10 says it is forbidden- they still continue to do it.
"I got plenty of liquor for the party tonight."
Master, how am I doin?
The slave masters gave the slaves liquor for the weekend after pickin' cotton.
"Man, that nigga is the truth!"
Master, how am I doin?
Falsehood of who we are as a people.
"Clinton was good to us, wasn't he master?"
Even though he hated on Obama calling him, Weak and "a puppet".
Saying he's not aggressive enough for the economy situation.
"Man I busted a cap in that nigga!"
Master, how am I doin?
Another Black Man dead.
"Man, I hit that bitch."
Master, how am I doin?

No respect for the Black Woman.

"Drugs in the Black Community, gold teeth, half dressed hoes, the finest drink, chrome on my ride, the bling bling, pants saggin', down low actions, gang bangin', incarcerated, another fatherless child, suicide, rape, molestation, hatin', robbin' one another and

B.E.T.- Black exploitation of tomorrow's youths."

Master, how am I doin?

Damn good, nigger.

Jennifer 'Jai' Washington

Is Ignorance Bliss?!

Inn-o-cence first known and remembered…
Birthed to queens dethroned; some surrendered…
> I didn't know I was black till I turned 13.

Lost in Coca-Cola/Mickey D sponsored girl scouts, while left
In Time Warner dictated 20 minute time-outs…
> I didn't know I was black till I turned 13.

Catholic skirts rammed dutifully down my throat…
Rich best friends, but damn, why am I broke?!
> I didn't know I was black till I turned 13.

Culture shock hit me hard…right around the time of puberty,
'Cause once I got this, this, and this; you no longer heard nor listened to
me.
> I didn't know I was black till I turned 13.

Identification lost in a Radio dial…
Assimilation became the targeted profile…
> I didn't know I was black till I turned 13.

Barbie & Ken were the role models for me…
But to realize I'm black meant that this could never REALLY be…
> I didn't know I was black till I turned 13.

This episode was one I surely must have missed;
'Cause Sesame Street NEVER, EVER, prepared me for this!
> I didn't know I was black till I turned 13.

Governed by racism & ruled by 'the Man's' bigotry…
I pledge allegiance to the flag & DAMN, I ain't even free!
                    I didn't know I was black till I turned 13.

Turned the other cheek 'cause that's what you preached,
But when I needed you; your cell said, "Out of Reach!"
                    I didn't know I was black till I turned 13.

Blessed with the color that brought forth all of civilization…
Cursed by the color that is hated by every nation…
                    I didn't know I was black till I turned 13.

Was it really only society's fault…that I fell…
through the cracks & was never mentioned nor caught?!
                    I didn't know I was black till I turned 13.

Hope wasn't lost! It never came on my block,
Crack cocaine took over…it's got that shit on lock!!
                    I didn't know I was black till I turned 13.

God is here…yes, I know NEVER sleeping…
But evil is legal; like cops, they got brothas creepin'!
                    I didn't know I was black till I turned 13.

The truth was hidden, like I said, it was always there.
Did I live a sheltered life or was it that you really just didn't care?!
                    I didn't know I was black till I turned 13.

I'm not hinting that this is good or bad…
For it wasn't a choice that I ever had.
                    I didn't know I was black till I turned 13.

I'm just going to quit 'cause you said no one would care if I ever told.
    I just wish someone had warned me before I turned a year old.

The 1ne 8ght Str8

No more slaps on the wrist.
Or claiming to be a victim from our nation being at-risk.
In fact, not one more excuse
because no longer are you still considered our "misguided youth".
See, they used to get mama on the phone
and when she showed up they'd send you on home.
Or they would release you after they filled you with fear.
After you had begged and pled and cried enough tears.
But today they didn't sit you inside of a holding cell.
They just cuffed you and then stuffed you inside of the jail
because you are eighteen now
and doing a grown man's crime
gets you a grown man's time.

Shawqui Y. Novoa

Wall Street

Stock. The Dow is up!
Trading! Trading! You must woo that uzi getting
your nosy peer shot down. Bang! Bang! He's dead.
Just another one of us put to sleep forever.
Umm.
Meanwhile, Jeep driving, a Lexus cruising, drive-by
shooting, videotape playing.
District Attorney giving indictments, the Governor signing
death warrants.
Our baby boys playing insanity.
Doctors prescribing more and more drugs to steal their
minds away, so there will be no more masterminds
like Sigmund Freud's. Just orange jump suits,
brown two-piece suits, and upstate boots.
Do they die on the street as warriors? Or become
warriors behind the tall cold brick wall of another world?
Wall street, Trading! Trading!
Is your investment stock or is it just to hold our brother back?
Trading! Trading!
Lock them away so there would be more building jails.
More and more cells. So you can cage them like
animals & number them like cattle. Yes! A time to
eat and a time to weep. Behind the tall cold walls.
Lawyers with their fake out. The tears of the mother.
See they cut through her. No, she can't hold him in
her arms! She can't feel the frightening that is inside
the little boy in this child. While she prays and asks
why? Meanwhile, the court crier said nothing you can
do mama, he has become a warrior of the stock trade.
Just a number in the system.

Feds got you on that illegal AK47
A.T.F. got you on that other firearm. The District
Attorney handing out indictments.
The Governor is giving death sentences
and signing the death warrants.

Nicole Williams

Disturbed Connotation

She listens.
Lyrical expression
of poverty;
urban life,
accompanied by
hip hop beats,
diamonds,
fast cars,
Moet.
She relates
dreams are the same.
For Us By Us
worn across
a small frame,
chest 32B, I think.
Strawberry silk
plaited
breathing life,
root to end.
We are similar.
Taste preferred
dark skin,
rap over rock.
Our exterior different.
Me, caramel.
Her, vanilla.

"What's up my Nigga"
She said.
I nod in reception.
We are contemporaries,
friends.

I think.

NIGGER

Is that all you see yourself as N----?
A N---- standing on a corner
complaining about there are no jobs
and not trying to do anything else.
Ass showing,
singing every Tupac, Biggie and Jay Z verse
but can't read to fill out a job application.
Is that all you see yourself as N----?
Or do you see yourself as a man
with his pants pulled up over his ass
with a buttoned down dress shirt on
going to fill out applications
or going to school to get your GED
or high school diploma
while still quoting every Tupac, Biggie and Jay Z verse?
Is that all you see yourself as N----?
Sitting around smoking blunt after blunt.
Drinking beer after beer
and shot after shot.
Then on the block
the next day bragging about how many drinks you had
and lying about the females you macked,
using lines and quotes from every rapper that made a movie.
Why don't you just settle down with one of your babies' mamas,
turn that green you smoking
into some green that buys groceries and pays bills.
Turn that beer into some milk for the kids to drink.
Turn that shot of liquor into some clothes so you won't have to worry about
baby mama drama.
Is that all you see yourself as?

I don't.

We are a Great Nation of Black People.

So, why not take all that knowledge you have about cooking up dope and attend college to become a chemist?

Take all that knowledge you have about how many grams are in a sack and become a math teacher.

I see all of us as the ruler of our own destination-

a race of Beautiful Black People;

not as the savages, killers and N----- as everyone else sees us.

So, I ask you, "Is that all you see yourself as?"

Young Black Prince

Time after time, I see prince after prince falling in waste.
Princes before me have even done the same.
The message has been selecting you and you still refuse to embrace it.
The dope game continues to be your angle.
Along with the exposure of thugness and pants saggin'- exposing the ass for an ole penitentiary invite.
Blood baths between each other; gothic murders of your own kind.
Jealousy and anger because you had no father in your zone.
So now you're confused; you like jails better than hotels.
You get mass tattoos to show hype; a copy of your tribal bloodline you were never taught.
You view true tribalism as savagery because you won't connect to your culture due to social blindness of black education.
You're gang related; Government hated.
Quick to kill your own; a Willie Lynch dedication to devilism
Like Father, like Son- penitentiary is better than college, Young Brother.
So you become lower than an animal; mentally challenged.
The caged bird sings; another lock up in progress.
Baby on the way- now you can't be there; either dead or in jail.
Then you get the nerve to make some more and brag about it.
Spoiled kid, look what you done did.
Getting sent back up for another five-plus bid.
Now you crackin' under pressure.
From dollar maker to big time snitch.
Peace be with you, young family.
You made your bed now you lie in it.
Everyone has their time, Young One- being wicked has a judgment to come.
Remember, Black Prince, lack of knowledge is a curse to your soul and your family.
In time, you will have nowhere to go except down.

Homosexuality is now stronger in your gender.
The Creator is exposing you, Young Prince.
You live by the gun- you die by the gun.
I pray for you, Young Prince, because tomorrow is never promised.
God wills it that you will do the right thing before it's too late.

"Redeem every firstborn child among your sons. When the time comes and your son asks you, 'What does this mean?' you tell him, 'GOD brought us out of Egypt, out of a house of slavery, with a powerful hand. When Pharaoh stubbornly refused to let us go, GOD killed every firstborn in Egypt, the firstborn of both humans and animals. That's why I make a sacrifice for every first male birth from the womb to GOD and redeem every firstborn son.' The observance functions like a sign on your hands or a symbol on the middle of your forehead. GOD brought us out of Egypt with a powerful hand."

It so happened that after Pharaoh released the people, God didn't lead them by the way through the land of the Philistines, which was the shortest route, for God thought, "If the people encounter war, they'll change their minds and go back to Egypt." So God led the people around by the desert road, looping around to the Red Sea. The Israelites left Egypt

THE NEO-REVOLUTIONARY
Black Community News Service

25 cents

THE BLACK PANTHER PARTY

Nicole Williams

Mis-Education of the N.I.G.G.A

We put our spin it.
We bend it, prolong the -a
in the way we say it.
We walk it, talk it,
act it and sometimes even be it.
We believe it empowers.
Took the negativity and made it ours.
Lack of knowledge in every sense of the word,
yet ignorance is what I've heard.
It's absurd,
our vision is blurred.
So fuck what you've heard,
don't address me with that word.
Don't present me the tranquility of the
word peace, then with lack of identity
disrespect my intelligence.
Internalized the hate of others,
forced it on my sisters and my brothers.
That word embraces those
of the Hip Hop community
even if they are a different color.
We still living in poverty,
Depression.
Fucked up reality of
oppression
still got me guessing and stressing.
Trying to get in where I fit in.
Got me asking myself questions, like,
is it because I'm black?
Is it because of the way I act?

Is it where I rest at?
Was I born it
and if I was born this way
am I supposed to die this way?
That same mind-set got me calling
my people bitches and hoes.
Spending all our money on
jewelry and clothes.
It isn't progressive to believe
we can change the connotation
especially when we got a
fixation with the word.
A declaration
of justification with the word.
Internalization phonetically
speaking of the word.
Affirmation is made throughout the
nation and played on every radio station
when the word is repetitious
on songs in heavy rotation.
Causing our children's communication
to become part of their termination
and without explanation they become slaves
to Hip Hop beats and
lyrics of damnation.
Retracting us back to that plantation.
That word implicates ignorance
and associates itself with the color black.
But being black does not equal ignorance
and stupidity is something I lack.
The value of our beauty
is reason enough to take
pride in ourselves and take our
communities back.
Get ourselves out this mental
jail and overstand
that intellectual liberation
is part of the equation.
Stop allowing ourselves to
repeat the word.
Stop the verbal persuasion and

believing that we as a people can change the
-ER to an -A and the denotation is now different.
Rap artists embrace the word
with an unapologetic twist,
while our counter parts in spite of everything
believe the connotation
of that word still exists.
You won't shackle my hands
with that word.
You won't enslave my mind
with a word that
binds my ancestry to lynchings
and hate crimes.
Self-hate crimes that now reflect these times.
You want me to embrace mine
with ignorant lines that don't
reflect the knowledge
attained by children's minds.
Sightless ... not able to see
that her skin is black and she bears
the burden just like me.
Sightless ... not able to see that he is black
and beautiful just like me.
And to the majority we have no authority,
we can be destroyed by calling ourselves
what most of the white world still considers
to be a minority;
a nigga.

Life Don't Respect Life

In my 40 years of living, I have seen more than some people my age and older have seen. I have seen more death than the grim reaper and Satan combined. The reason I am writing this is because I am ready to see life. I mean real life. I know that there will always be death- that is part of life. But what I am saying is, can we as people- as human beings- respect life to the fullest? Can we give the elders their respect first and foremost? My generation and the next one behind me doesn't have any respect. I have never seen such disrespect; not only to each other, but to ourselves as well. We need to get back to having the kids going out to the trees and bushes and pick their own switches for discipline. What about the way that young people are dressing? Too big and baggy. Or too tight and short. There is no respect for their personal appearance and hygiene. Should we just blame society and forget about the parents? We should blame both because it takes a village to raise a King and Queen. But first, we have to teach and show them how to be princes and princesses. Not to look for guidance in negative people and things but by taking pride in them; showing them how to respect themselves and others. There is no excuse now that we have a Black President. We as Black people are under a microscope and times are not going to get any easier. Times are only going to get harder. This is no time to get lazy. It means to keep on pushing, baby. Life should not be ending at age 13, 14 or even 15 years old. It is just the beginning and you should be striving to be the next Black President. Life. It's your choice. Respect it.

Jäe ki-Moja

The Future is to be Seen

Children have ideas
but our minds are shut.

Children's mouths open
but people shut them closed.

"Children are our future"
they all say.
But then it's
a word to the wise ...
"Children are to be seen; not heard."

So, two more words to the wise ...
"Always listen to the future" and
"Never be hypocritical."

Disconnect

I remember adult protestors to the P-Funk All Stars and white boys playing that funky music. Not understanding our zeal for atomic dogs, Mary Jane, or getting funked up and down all night long.

Realizing later that despite our musical tastes that decade, we were listening. We understood.

The struggle, the blessings, how far you'd come.

Now there is a disconnect.

Not just in the music our children listen to, in all its blaring, audacious, insensitivity. Can nothing be left to our imaginings anymore?

The poetic rap masters that Grandmaster ushered in have gotten lost, leading our children with them. Confused as to the point of the rhyme.

The ingenious flow of Biggie, just tellin' his story and Ice Cube, just keeping it real became tarnished by obscene trash with no substance, no meaning, no heart.

Our children are lost and don't seem to recognize the sound of our voice leading them home. We must talk louder.

We must go to the mountain tops and steadily proclaim Martin's sacrifices, Malcolm's pride, Emmett's courage, Ali's conviction, Shirley's boldness, Marcus' strength, Barack's determination, and Sojourner's Truth.

We must reconnect them to their past so they understand the urgency of the present.

Grab them and hold them long and hard. Insist they give back. Teach them to serve so they begin to appreciate.

MAKE THEM UNDERSTAND!

So they no longer settle for being debased and degraded.

So they no longer strive for mediocrity.

It is our greatest task and it will be our greatest triumph, connecting our children back to their beginning so they can be reconnected to themselves.

The Listening

Some folks are out here sleep walking,
while others keep talking;
having these conversations between the ignorant and the uncaring
as they begin daring
to debate the dumb,
deaf,
and blind
over what is troubling mankind
whereby
our old plantation lullabies
become those contemporary urban concertos
that can be heard playing in the ghettos
and seen played out in the most ironic portrayals
of suffering, death, and betrayal.
Unscripted
but only to those who need to be uplifted
because the most righteous of the rebels
are WE who rebelled,
rioted,
and resisted
by posing enough opposition
to cause the People to stand up and listen.

Shawqui Y. Novoa

The Silent Cry

I have been young and have heard the cry of many . . .
A weep of sorrow a weep of pain,
the cry of a child when someone takes from it a penny,
a holler- a scream, until help came.
Even the cry of a baby is pacified . . .
whether by the suggestion of a discomfort,
or by the starry-glazed eyes,
assistance is given, because of the cry.
There is a land where the cry is not heard . . .
tears have dried up, heads are no more fallen down,
helplessly existing-with very little aid from man,
but God has filled their cup and taken away their frown.
A survival instinct intensifies the air . . .
a need to eat, a need to be educated,
a need to be cared for, a burden to share.
For many years their cry went out . . .
from sea to shining seas all throughout the land,
only a few heard the shout.
Yet very few did understand.
Now their cry is silent . . .
only those who can truly understand will hear,
and we must cry out for them,
so that the once sorrowful tears may become joyful tears.

Night

Night is my favorite time of day.
With its cool blackness, night engulfs you and gently rocks your soul.
Night beats with the rhythmic pulse of an ancient, tribal drum.
Steady, strong, constant.
Night hears the cries and sees the blood
of the man-child that lived too fast and died too young.
Night is Black like me.
Cool and strong like.
Night feels like me.
Night is my favorite time of day.

Shawqui Y. Novoa

Echoes on the street

Echoes of voices. Echoes of voices whispering through the crowds of people. Sounds of tat, tat, tat, tat.

There goes that 9mm smoke filling the air like a smoke bomb was there.

Cell phones, beepers- who calls? 9mm strap like tat, tat, tat. Meanwhile, Jeep driving ... Infinity cruising. Cell phones ringing- who there?

Beepers blinking. 9mm ready-ready-ready automatic under the seats. Coke filled bottle blunts... Feeling soooooooooooooo cool. A pack of Newport's on the seat. Music blasting. Knowing all the words!

Lights out...here they come! Bang ... bang. She dead.

His brain lying over there all alone. She's shot in the chest, her body jumps like zap, zap. While blood pours, though her blouse, grasping for air, her last breath. Someone call 9-1-1. The sound of the rescue squad was near. Bang ... bang. They're dead. Walk away- who cares?

They were once here now they're gone. They left a mark. Ummmmmmmmmmmm.

A mark here like a street name. Candles ... candles.

Nightfall has come. Vigil cards.

Flowers and more flowers were like an outdoor funeral. Mark the place, we'll be back. The rescue squad carries them away. Crime scene. Did everyone see? Homicide here, Yellow tape?

While smoke still fills the air with this foul odor. Odor of death shells. Shells lay everywhere, like picking up candy. Ummmmmmmmmmmmmm.

Meanwhile, crack vials intersperse with the shells.

Blood painted the pavement red. The tears, the last heart beat, the screaming.

Help. Help that echoes of a cry, the deep tears. The crowd's fears upon everyone's faces.

Face of fear.

Face of fear.

Face of a brother.

Face of a brother of someone.

A once was. A once was a beautiful face.

A smiling face.

Never again.

Just a face at this place.

Echoes…

Echoes of a voice.

Whispering through the crowd.

Just echoes on the streets.

FIVE

WE, the People, can then begin to change things through our revolution.

Like Wolves

John F. Kennedy once said, "A revolution is coming- a revolution which will be peaceful if we are wise enough; compassionate if we care enough; successful if we are fortunate enough- but a revolution which is coming whether we will it or not. We can affect its character, we cannot alter its inevitability."

That revolution will overthrow the capitalist system.

Now it is important to note that America is a capitalist nation and capitalism has two classes. If you subscribe to socialist thought then you will refer to them as: the ruling class and the proletariat; that is, the aristocracy and the working class.

The two classes that are often referred to as the *haves* and the *have-nots*.

Many of you have been duped into believing that you have made it and that you are living the American Dream, so, you consider yourselves to be middle class. However, I ask you to consider the premise of the shrinking middle class that has been recently reported on the news. It is from this group that you currently see the numbers of unemployed and underemployed people increasing. More people from this group are applying for government assistance, filing bankruptcy, and going to food banks now. And the greatest increase in crimes is being committed by this group- your American middle class.

Now, when it was just the *have-nots* doing things like committing crimes, filing bankruptcy, and going to food banks you called it survival because those are some of the things that must be done in order to survive. But it is no different in any other case. If you are not a member of the ruling class then you are in survival mode whether you think you are middle class or not! While you may not have filed bankruptcy, perhaps you have considered it.

Maybe you are living from one paycheck to the next and you are dodging the collection calls. While you may not be committing any crimes per se, maybe you routinely rob from Peter and pay it out to Paul in order to make ends meet. And even if you have never gone to a food bank, let's consider the fact that you fancy yourself a spendthrift who frugally shops for bargains in the various supermarkets. You settle for the most economical cuts of meat but you know that elsewhere in America there are wealthier people who indulge themselves on the most prime, choicest cuts of meat that are much too pricy for you to enjoy.

This is because capitalism in America only has two classes. The middle class is not shrinking because there never was a middle class. The establishment allowed you to believe that the fruits of your labors had elevated you to a new class; one lying above that of the proletariat class. But this was only an illusion; a middle class illusion that was created to serve as a buffer between the ruling class and the proletariat. It gave you a false sense that you had gotten somewhere in life in order to keep you pacified. They threw you a bone and you mistakenly thought that you were going to eat for life. The elite dine on the best cut of the meat and then they throw you the bone. How can anyone expect to feed off of a bone?

Consider what is said in Ezekiel 22:27 which reads, "Your leaders are like wolves who tear apart their victims. They actually destroy people's lives for money!"

In return, you do their bidding by barking and howling loud enough to keep the others who are hungry among you quiet. You say, "Look at me. I'm an example of someone who has pulled himself up by his bootstraps ..." because you think that you are middle class and you have made it to your American Dream. You think you are a wolf just like the rest of those wolves in the ruling class. What you do not realize is how damaging your professed bootstrap ideology actually is to us as a people. It serves to keep us divided.

The nightmarish reality of America sets in when you look up and you see the establishment taking the very same bone from your mouths. But it was never yours. It was the ruling class who gave you that job. That house came to you along with a mortgage that was held by the elite. The car was leased to you by the aristocrats and now they want it all back. You didn't even own that pair of boots that they allowed you to wear. Now you try pulling yourself up by those same bootstraps but you cannot; just like so many other people in the so-called American middle class who lost everything in stock market crashes, corporate down-sizing, or real estate foreclosures.

You look around and you're still just as hungry as the rest. Now you're back in survival mode again. It is survival of the fittest. But if you survive, will you be fooled by them again?

There is no middle class here in America but as long as you allowed yourself to believe that you were somehow different from the rest of the working class, you never thought of our problems as your problems. Class is defined in terms of whether you are the owner of the means to acquire wealth, by what role you play in the production of that wealth, and by what share of that wealth you receive. So, what is this middle class and exactly where would it fit within a system where you either own the means to acquire wealth or you do not?

See, what you and I need is a revolution. The problem we both have is that you haven't realized this yet.

According to the foreword in George Jackson's book entitled <u>Soledad Brother</u>, "Of course, when it finally becomes more attractive for one to fight, and perhaps die, than to live in a survival mode, a revolution starts to become a possibility."

And the first step to realizing the need for revolution can be made by taking an honest, eye-opening look at the capitalist system. Does its ruling class more closely resemble you and the people you know who are most like you? Or would that be the proletariat? Which class is disproportionately unemployed or under-employed in low paying jobs? Which class faces widespread deficits in education in addition to facing systemic efforts at suppressing any learning of culture and heritage that differs from the dominant culture? Who is more routinely denied access to adequate health care and social services? Do the people who are brutalized by the police and imposed upon by questionable laws and policies resemble the ruling class or the working class?

We need a revolution that involves everyone who is oppressed against our oppressors in the ruling class to bring a radical reordering of wealth, resources, and priorities. A revolution that excludes neither men, women, nor youth by means of classism, chauvinism, or racism. We need a revolution that is inclusive of you.

Now, you may look at yourself in materialistic terms and because of your accumulated wealth, you may still believe that things are somehow different for you because you were able to acquire this thing or that. Regardless of the points that I make here, you think the things you have surely must place you into some sort of middle class. On the contrary, bear in mind the likelihood that you have merely been given access to credit where others were not. Whether this is true because of your debt to income ratio, credit rating, level of education attained, or skin color, somehow, you were deemed credit worthy in a way that others had not been. And you believe that makes you middle class now. Well, you must also be mindful that the system of capitalism has the same power to take that away from you in return. Recent events and history has demonstrated this through the lowering of credit limits, the strengthening of the criteria to gain credit, and the repossession of capital based on the creditor's perception of your inability to repay it on their terms.

Our society is one that consists of the land owners and the landless. This is a key point that Malcolm X addresses in his *A Message to the Grassroots* speech. There is no third class of people in the middle. And to those of you who happen to be landlords, you still need to realize that in a capitalist system the banks and finance companies truly own that land until you have paid it off; until that happens you are in a sense landless as well.

So, if you are someone who is in survival mode, then what you and I need is a revolution. If you are stuck in a low paying job, then what you and I need is a revolution. But if the loss of your high paying job has forced you back out into the job market, then what you and I need is a revolution. And if you are suffering from deficits in the education you received, then what you and I need is a revolution. You and I need a revolution if you are homeless and disenfranchised. Or if you have a house but it is up for foreclosure, then what you and I need is a revolution. In short, if you have been denied access to the American Dream, then what you and I need is a revolution.

Staci Celeste

Change

Colored Rest Room
That's the sign that hangs over my daddy's couch in his den.
Snatched down from the black boys bathroom door and
pissed on during his college days.
Pee stains still apparent along the rusted edges.
The message's sting has faded though.
We're black now.
Black and beautiful.
Black and proud.
My mamaw was dark black.
105 she live to be; born when her brown eyes dared not meet blue or green
ones directly.
She bleached and bleached that black skin.
That stubborn, thick, resilient skin stayed black.
Stayed Black.
She would laugh out loud to see our new president.
Our wide nose, thick lipped, true African Black Man president.
Black man president.
Black man president.
It's here, just like the good book always promised, the change.
The change has come.
Not the first, not the last.
Sit in front, not in back.
Shine pretty chocolate girl, shine.
Reach for the top genius black boy, reach.
Yes you can be all you can be.
Yes you will be all you can be.
Yes you must be all you can be.

Hustler's Creed

Trying daily
to capitalize on a system that could enslave me. I
find "hustling" is a street entrepreneur's way of getting paid.
A Hustler's Creed; game set in stone. It's
easier to advance when you take the game **mental** and leave the bullshit alone.
Legal or illegal: Have more invested in your "**hustle**" than a public defender.
Way to survive: Learn from game that's getting sheisty all the time. And always remember **to** recognize game, you **must** know **how to** use it!
Make a habit of taking no L's (losses) because a **buttflosser** is what the **game** will have you confused with!
Money hungry "dummies" work **for** money Monday through Sunday!
Without a **game plan** like a **savings plan**, get used to looking **serious** like Al Bundy.
Working for money is what Society wants you to do. If your "**re-up**" ain't no "**come-up**" your money ain't working **for** you.
For attention just like envy is sown into the seams of every hustler's game.
It separates The "**Hustlers**" from the "**Busters**." The "**Doers**" from the "**Lames**". Who will **always** complain (PH'n)
Make no moves without knowing what you have to lose. Have "Dream Team" money set **aside** in case **they** come for you.
Your techniques always show in your speech. A Real Hustler looks twice before they speak or reach. For
money is only "**loyal to**" & "**respects**" the "**few**" that know like they show how to collect it – stretch it – stack it!
Work like you hustle, **Hustle** like you work and expect everyone who ain't "**like you**" to attack this.

For a Hustler, "success is not a destination but a journey. True Hustlers learn how to **lead**, following the game plans of **O.G.s** who **don't advertise** what they do with their cheese.

You should always be wary of folks who just want to join your team. Read the 1st word of every line & you'll have the **Hustler's Creed**.

Critic All

The blatant exploitation
of millions in the ultimate pyramid scheme
called capitalism;
a corrupted economic system
backed by and empowered with the politicism
of soldiers,
laws,
prisons,
police,
and more politics.
So, the system should be drowning in the blood of the People.
Instead, the sequel
to the American promise for our emancipation
merely brought about a change in the form of our exploitation.
But the People need more than a change in the name
and only a critical resistance can bring about a radical change.

See, political power also flows from the ballpoint of a pen.

Darren Reed

Good Morning America

The night was long,
four hundred years-plus long,
they prayed dawn would
greet me.

Bodies and fears were
lost in the night,
and the night was long,
four hundred years-plus long.

Traces of cold night
flow like the Nile
in my veins,
for the journey was not
in vain.

Through resilient eyes
I speak words of the
night travelers unable to
utter sounds of freedom.

I am a seed
planted on that night,
and the night was long
four hundred years-plus long.

Dawn greets me kindly today,
brilliant sun in my eyes.
I am the destination.

With pride I speak for
the unspoken.

Good morning America,
the journey has arrived.

So BE It

If WE be the vanguard,
then so be it.

And if there is imminent danger,
then so be it.

And if WE make waves
that turn the troubled waters muddy,
then so be it.

And if our revolution turns bloody,
then so be it.

And if they will call US terrorist,
then so be it.

And if America is scared of it,
then so be it.

Recognize Game!

Fourth quarter, 2 minute warning, whistle being played. Our team's song, **"We Shall Overcome!"** is no longer being displayed. Who are my safeties? Is my team's defense going to save me? Or that brother running for the touchdown?

"**Malcolm's been shot!**" **First Down!** Time out, Time out ... Huddle on the line. What we gone do? They got coach.

Who are we supposed to listen to? Time running out. Somebody call the next play! And no more turnovers to "endorsements" that got our "**team**" looking the other way! If you're on this field facing this way ... You better play!

There goes the whistle. **Let's go, team!**

Hut 1, Shot 1 ...

"**Somebody sacked the Dream!**" **Second Down!**

Get up, Martin! The play was just starting ... who we got to play third string? Oh y'all just gone quit the **team**? Together we were standing. Team now divided some of y'all changing jerseys for the other side. Those sideline commercials got some of us saying "**cheese**" to the opposing teams. Are they playing us like rivalries or enemies? Are we supposed to be playing like a **team** or just **enemies**? Every time we get some **unity** we catch a **penalty**?

(**Recognize Game!**)

Penalty!? Four hundred year loss of yardage line of scrimmage back on the twenty! Down by two! 2 Pac you know what we need to do! Go long baby, **Keep ya head up! All eyes on me, on three!** And when you get it baby, **Smile for me!** Hut 2, Hut 3 ... **M.V.T.** Makaveli, where you be? Wide open and I'm **Tossin it up** to thee!

"**First & 20**" But how'd he go down with blood on his jersey? This don't make sense! "Time out ... Time out!" Yo! Where was his defense?

Dear Mama: Dry your eyes. Some of my teammates don't know how to **Recognize Game!** We've been **free agency** since **slavery** or are we slaves to a shcisty "**field nigga**" mentality? "**Nothing to live for.**" "**Nothing to play for.**" "**Nothing to do.**" No fears of dying. Why bother trying? The next blitz is lining up for **who**?

This game is real (why you playin'?!) It's not one of those made for T.V. Dramas. Especially when they sack your quarterback. But why do our leaders, I mean our **wide receivers**, keep ending up **on their backs**? Is unsportsman like behavior the only way we get advertised as saviors? Maybe that's why we have to share a locker room with **Players** and **Haters**.

You mean that white lipstick and a watermelon dance won't save you? I wonder if I look in the mirror … You'd probably see who just "played you!" What you gonna do? What are we going to do? Because I'm tired of explaining & displaying to the kids we're "**really losing too!**" "**Maybe next year**" or that **nigga wild card** is good enough for you, but I laced up to win this game today! Because we were never televised but advertised as the underdogs. We were the **NEGRO LEAGUE**. But check your mirror, the revolution is starting to appear; the **All New Expansion Team**!

So let the media yell, "May the Revolution fail!" May the **Revolution succeed**! **Game recognized Game** and you can always run game on "**lames**". How many more losses in the History books do **you** plan to continue to claim???

Down by 3, 1ˢᵗ and 20 (Here's the play by play) **3x120** ……………….. **Recognize Game!**

Say Blood (Believe That)

Black Panther blood got spilled
when Bobby Hutton got killed …
and there was the shooting
of Huey P. Newton …
and H. Rap Brown
got put on lock down …
and Bobby Seale
and Angela Davis
endured incarceration …
and George Jackson's assassination …
along with the prison abuses suffered
by the Soledad Brothers
as the brothers up in Attica
stood up and threw down spectacular …
Then John Huggins
and Alprentice Carter
were victims of manslaughter
on the UCLA campus
but WE understand that was
from COINTELPRO provocation …
Just like Fred Hampton's assassination …
And the exile of Eldridge Cleaver …

Man, that's what made me a believer.

Ghetto Messiah

The world turns its gaze
towards inner cities set ablaze
from a world consumed in hatred, pain, grief, and shame.
WE need only look in a mirror to find someone to blame.

But through the outrage and fire
the ghetto calls for a Messiah
as WE beseech and implore
for deliverance
because imprisoned
are the People yearning
The fires are still burning
in places like Los Angeles, Chicago, Newark, Cincinnati,
Cleveland, Richmond, Detroit, and Miami.
And stormy is the underground weather
threatening the longest, hottest summers ever
because WE cannot hide the scars on our backs
that chattel slavery has left on US Blacks.
And too much of her is ugliness-
although she is called America the Beautiful.
So, what you should know
is that the winds are turning
and the fires are still burning.
Like being locked away inside of a cage
and feeding on nothing but rage
for years and years.
WE need a Ghetto Messiah to deliver our mothers from the tears
that are shed over sons lost;
a payment in blood for the violence that our guns cost.
Come deliver our brethren from their cells.

No longer shall they rot away inside of jails.
Come deliver our sisters.
Come deliver our children.
Let US inherit the Earth and start rebuilding.

Khamin abu-Jäe

Where Are the Revolutionaries?

At the end of the Public Enemy music video *Shut 'Em Down*, Chuck D gazes at graffiti left on a wall in order to pose us with a question. The wall reads: "Where are the revolutionaries?"

A widely held misconception is that most of the revolutionaries are either locked up or dead. Because this appears to be a fact at first glance, a deeper examination is needed.

Inarguably, many young people are lost today because we are suffering from a lack of leadership in our communities. Nowadays, participation in street gangs and other types of widespread thuggery seems to be commonplace within the cities where our people reside. Also, there is a connection between what many consider thuggish behavior and some behaviors that are common to the revolutionary. In either scenario, we find disenfranchised people who want change and oppose the system in order to get it. However, without proper, constructive leadership the opposition usually poses a detriment to our communities.

To illustrate this, the documentary film *Bastards of the Party* directed by Antoine Fuqua upholds the premise that the Los Angeles' Bloods and Crips street gangs arose to their current levels of prominence because the people found themselves leaderless in the aftermath when key Black Panther Party members had been slain or imprisoned. Left behind were the masses of leaderless, disenfranchised people. Again, without the proper leadership their efforts to make things happen became destructive rather than constructive; they became a detriment to the community instead of being a benefit. Given this as fact, what happened in Los Angeles is merely a microcosm for what has happened all across America during the late twentieth century. By examining street gangs in cities like New York and Chicago, we witness the very same response to very similar circumstances. In fact, what happened in New York,

Los Angeles, and Chicago has taken place in urban centers throughout the United States and is even occurring in suburban and rural locations today.

See, the revolutionaries are already in place. There is no doubt that our communities are filled with people who are already opposing the system in order to change things. What is missing is our revolutionary leadership. This was true in Los Angeles when Al "Bunchy" Carter used his leadership of the Slausons to reorganize the gang into politically radical groups following the Watts Riots. Later, many other Bloods-affiliated gangs would begin to follow suit. Some may argue that Stan "Tookie" Williams and Ray Washington did the same with the Crips. Whether considered as constructive or destructive, the leadership that they provided is undeniable. In Chicago, that same type of leadership could be seen as Jeff Fort and Eugene Hairston united numerous west-side youth into gangs like the Black P-Stones, Vice Lords, and other gangs allied under the Peoples Nation. Likewise, the Gangster Nation led by Larry Hoover and David Barksdale's Disciples unified south-side youths into the Folks. Moreover, this is no different than what Gustavo Colon did with the Latin Kings for Hispanic youth in Chicago. Again, whether these gangs became detrimental to their communities aside, no one can argue that the leadership was not present along with a critical mass of people who were ready to oppose the establishment.

In many cases, their leadership was very constructive. For instance, Bunchy Carter would eventually become a key figure in much of what the Black Panther Party was able to accomplish in Watts and Los Angeles. In Chicago, Bobby Gore led the Conservative Vice Lords in working with community based activists in order to bring about several local economic and political improvements. Also in Chicago, Fred Hampton used his leadership to further the efforts of the NAACP and the Black Panther Party. In addition, he was able to secure an unprecedented truce between historically rival gangs and boost membership in the Black Panther Party. Jose Jimenez and Felipe Luciano organized Puerto Ricans in Chicago and Spanish Harlem into the Young Lords Party, which often aligned itself alongside the Black Panther Party in their efforts to benefit their communities. Sonny Carson worked to reform former members of Brooklyn street gangs into a movement called the New Republic of Afrika. The leadership of George Jackson was key in the founding of the Black Guerilla Family and the formation of the Third World Coalition, an advocacy organization for prison reform.

These facts are all congruent with two common premises of in many of the poems in <u>Until Uhuru: For US Colored Folks</u>. First of all, there are many people amongst us who are anti-establishment and they want change to things. Secondly, we can use the same energy that our people already possess but we must channel it differently.

The contingency for our efforts being beneficial and constructive to our communities hinges on providing the masses with the proper leadership. Again, the revolutionary spirit is already present within those who want to change our political system, criminal justice practices, and economic policies. What we lack is the revolutionary leadership.

It is one thing to rebel against the system at large, but modern society considers the rebel without a cause as nothing more than a thug or hooligan whose behaviors are detrimental to their community. In contrast, the historical view that society has for the rebel is often romanticized as someone who is very noble for having the determination to oppose a system that is unjust. The difference between the methodologies of these two types of rebels often rests on the leadership that they receive.

So, the question is not "where are the revolutionaries?" so much as it should be "where is the revolutionary leadership?"

Well, we can find our answer looking right back at us in our mirrors. We are out on the streets hustling and struggling to make it. But we are also out on the streets in the midst of the people being visible in our efforts to helping the masses change things. We are also working in the schools impacting young minds and opening their eyes by fostering the discourse between students and teachers. We are in the barbershops and beauty parlors and nail salons holding dialogue and heated debate filled with critical thought. We are also working inside of the courts and social service agencies helping to positively impact lives rather than surrendering those valuable lives to the system. We are at the universities and on the street corners applying practice to our theories. We are out in the marketplaces, down in the pool halls and recreation centers, up in the church houses and temples, over in the corner bars and coffee houses as well as in the libraries and bookstores preparing for a revolution that will constructively benefit our communities. The revolutionaries are wherever there are people who want to take their rage, aggression, and ambition and then channel it to make constructive changes by means of social activism. As revolutionary leaders, we must step forward and help to lead them.

2 Mao Tse-tung

My quest called knowledge for answers
to questions ranging from the Black Panthers
all the way back to our ancestors
had me reading everything from <u>Assata</u>
to <u>Soledad Brother</u>,
<u>Soul On Ice</u>, and others.
Now revolution flows from the ballpoint of my pen
as if it were the barrel of a gun.
But that seems to be a peril for some
and a threat to the establishment.
Buck the status quo as they wonder where the status went
and the grassroots followed by example as they were led
by comrades Huey, Eldridge, Angela, and Fred
on the path to survival and subsistence
through critical thought and resistance
to break beyond the barriers and harsh looks
holding up Little Red Books in one hand
and raised Black fists in the other.

So, I got down with the Movement
for my sisters and brothers.

Instant Replay (for Malcolm X)

In an instant, it all flashed past him
as he stood before the Audubon Ballroom.

How he would use an X
to represent the unknown
when Malcolm Little
had become too small …
when the reputation of Big Red
had been killed dead
from playing
part pimp,
part thug,
part hustler …

How prison brought out the best in some
while others were ruined completely …
How he wondered which one would he be?
How he would sit in that jail
locked inside of his cell …
How he would look backwards
on Harlem, heroin, hustlers and hookers …
How he would look forwards
towards Muhammad, Mecca, and the Muslims …

How there would be confusion …

How he wanted to submit to Allah but could not …
How he used to get down on his knees to pick open a lock …

How he would come to understand why his father had followed Marcus
Garvey ...

How he would see a divine apparition ...
How the Honorable Elijah Muhammad would come to him in a vision ...
How he would then be able to kneel to something greater than himself ...
How he would submit his will to something so much greater than himself ...

How he would come to know
Allah the Beneficent,
Allah the Merciful,
Allah the –

And it was at that very instant,
when El-Hajj Malik El-Shabazz looked into the eyes of his assassins ...
but he would not see hate
nor even death.

He would finally see peace.

4 the People

As Black Power
and a new Leftist age converged,
a counter cultural revolution emerged
into a movement for radical social change
with some key persons named
Mao, Marx, and Lenin,
Malcolm X and Ho Chi Mihn,
Che Guevara
and Nkrumah
with cultural nationalists like
Baraka and Karenga
pointing an accusatory finger
as Kennedy, Khrushchev, and Castro
took US all to the brink of disaster
while Dr. King
was brave enough to dream
for the People.

POWs

Media falsehoods tell US that
"America has no political prisoners"-
Bullshit.
Many of US get held as hostages of the pulpit
or as prisoners of the war on drugs.
With our politicians playing the role of thugs,
WE are all like political prisoners in this war on poverty.
And it bothers me
that WE have declared war
on the disenfranchised and poor
then WE pray to the God of the oppressed
for our exploitations to be addressed.
Foreign aid packages?
Or for an AIDS package?
Utilizing chemical and biological warfare tactics
like syphilis for the Black man,
and small pox for the Indians,
with my People on the front lines from the very beginning and
government inspired social mechanics
like H1N1 and swine flu mist;
same as lethal injections.
Lethal infections of AIDS/HIV
A human manufactured disease of epidemic proportions.
WE proceed but with caution
WE wrestled with rampant alcohol abuse,
AIDS/HIV,
and intravenous drug use.
Our communities flooded
with crack cocaine,
heroin,

and methamphetamine.
Y'know what I mean?
But revolutionary chaos,
bedlam, and mayhem
boasts the promises
for the rebirth of a bold new world.
Despite this cold, cruel world
holding US captive
as its prisoners of war.

There is no true justice, freedom, or equality
here in America. Man has imposed himself upon the
will of The Almighty leaving justice only to those
who can afford to pay the highest for it. Freedom
only comes at a price and, therefore, it is not
free. And what has equality ever meant in this
land unless you were a white man who owned land?

America is the Modern Babylon. Those
twin World Trade Center Towers, a
capitalist symbol for commerce, greed,
and corruption have fallen. So did the
Tower of Babel.

America must acknowledge, amend, and atone for her atrocities!

Unite Until Uhuru

The proverbial burning spear has been thrust into the ground,
so, brothers and sisters, it's time to get down.

WE join together
from Angola, Louisiana
and from the country of Angola …

WE join together
from the country of South Africa,
and from numerous countries in South America, and
WE join from the former slave holding states of the American south …

WE join together
from countries along the African savannah
and from Savannah, Georgia …

WE join together
from every corner of the globe
painted a shade of Black by the African Diaspora
for our requiem of blood, sweat, and tears
invested over the years
as WE now fight for unity
through the freedom, independence, and liberty
of Black folks; one and all.

WE join together
as my People cry out and call,
"Unite until Uhuru!"

Biographies

Ali Bilal is from Philadelphia, PA. Because he grew up the youngest child in a house filled with talented artists, Ali Bilal pushed himself to excel as he competed for recognition amongst his family at an early age. However, he did not begin writing until late during his teenage years. Now his writings and artwork often encompass well-known figures involved such as Assata Shakur, Che Guevara, and other revolutionaries because he identifies with their struggle. He also writes introspectively on Black love and the many lessons that life has for us to learn.

Taya R. Baker is a judicial assistant for the DeKalb County State Court in GA, as well as a DeKalb County Court Appointed Special Advocate by day; by night she is a poet and a published author. To her credit she has one published novel, <u>Every Time I Close My Eyes</u>, released in 2003. She also has two unpublished novels, <u>Daddy's Big Girl</u> and <u>Sold Sister</u>. <u>Every Time I Close My Eyes</u> continues to receive positive reviews and continues to be requested by book club readers. Because of the cross appeal of her first novel, Taya has traveled throughout the southeastern states as a guest author at book clubs, middles schools and high schools. She is also working on a book of poetry, <u>Amongst Friends</u>. She quotes poet Mark Strand: *"Ink runs from the corners of my mouth. There is no happiness like mine. I have been eating poetry."*

Jai Braden is currently living in Atlanta, GA by way of East Cleveland, OH. She is writing a crime/romance novel tentatively entitled <u>Karma</u>. *"Ambition without authenticity will spoil the riches."*

C-G.R.I.T.S. has her deepest roots set in Memphis, TN. Her moniker is an acronym which stands for County Girl Raised in the South. She has been writing since her teenage years and she began writing as a way of finding self-expression and creative release. Her adage is: *"**Aspire to inspire before you expire.**"*

Staci Celeste is originally from Dayton, OH but Cincinnati has been her home for the last decade. A mother, teacher, lover, fighter, writer, and friend, Staci enjoys creating anything that produces peace. Her poetic debut was made at *Mahogany Soul*. She has always been passionate about her writing. As a result, she has not only dabbled in poetry but in children's books, love stories and some humorous "reality" spins on her world as an educator and mother as well. She holds a Master of Education from Xavier University and she has recently completed a collection of poems entitled <u>Pieces of Me</u>. Only God comes before her children and family and she credits her imagination, talent, inspiration and any successes to Him. Her life motto is: *"**Live your passion and the peace will follow.**"*

Dawn Crooks is a native of Cincinnati, OH, currently residing in the New York City metro area. She obtained a BA in English Literature from Central State University in 1997. Dawn is a college administrator by profession; a job that allows her to exercise her passion for mentoring youth. She is a poet, a spoken word performance artist, and fiction writer by trade, and an activist at her core. She has also developed two workshops for youth: one on issues of self-esteem, respect, honoring life and nurturing their temples, and the other is about the images of men and women in Hip Hop. She has also developed a performance workshop that teaches the techniques of spoken word performance art.

The middle child of three, Dawn was an only girl, which often left her to her own creative devices for entertainment. Her passion for writing developed out of this seclusion and she has been writing ever since the age of 11 when she first realized that writing gave her a voice, a presence, and power to transcend her loneliness. In fact, she penned her first novella in the sixth grade, entitled <u>Teenage Blues</u>. Although an unpublished work, it was complete with a book cover and illustrations. Dawn was afforded the opportunity to share it with her classmates, from which her passion for performance was born. On stage, her name is Wisdom and she is seasoned at the spoken word craft, having hosted several open mic events, including *The Vibe* with DJ Perry Simmons, and performed in a host of featured performances throughout her career for churches, sororities and fraternities and other student organizations, as well for numerous community based organizations. Dawn is currently working diligently towards her lifetime goals of becoming a full-time, published poet and novelist, and an inspirational speaker.

Dawn says this about her love for poetry and what serves as her poetic muse: *"I have been having a love affair with words for as long as I can remember. It is this adoration that fuels my creativity and passion for writing poetry and for performing. I have to write. The pull inside of me to create won't allow me to do anything other than compose. When it comes to writing, I respect work that has a purpose, that is cleverly written, that goes beyond the common, that inspires truth, and that is artsy and soulful and can touch a heart and move a spirit in a way that gets down into your center, plants its feet and grows legs, and causes such a stir that you are forever changed. That is exactly what I want my poetry, fiction and performances to do. No matter where you want to go, I want my words to be able to take you there!"*

Michael J. Crump grew up in Dayton, OH. He has been writing and reciting his poetry for about two years. Sometimes called the Mikrophone Check, many of his contemporaries at the *Lyrical Insurrection* have accepted him as one of their "brothers-in-rhyme". He firmly believes that: *"Fatherhood is defined by how your children respect their elders. Fatherhood is displayed by integrity, respect, honesty, and love."*

D Quest 4 Knowledge was raised in Chicago, IL and he moved to Cincinnati, OH in 1999. Although this father of three has been writing poetry for years, he just began sharing his gift with a few over the past five years. *"My poems in this book will give me God's blessings of sharing my talent with everyone. Hope you enjoy..."*

Desmond Storm E Jones currently resides in Columbus, OH. He is an actor, poet, public speaker, entrepreneur, filmmaker, and author. A personal mission of his is to combine these five disciplines in order to promote individual and social understanding through theater in the community. Storm E does a lot of this through his creative multimedia business, Eye of the Storm Production works.

As an actor, Storm E has chosen roles that reflect the diversity of African Americans to positively impact the community. Noteworthy performances include his roles in August Wilson's *Fences* and *Race* by Jamie Pachino, which addresses the American obsessions for race, discrimination, and inequality. Storm E took the lead role in the documentary film *After the 16th*, which focused on the after effects of the Million Man March. He also played in *Fools,* a comedy by Neil Simon. As part of Cleveland Public Theater's 16th Annual New Plays Festival 1998- "Sex, Politics, and Religion", he was in three plays: *The Watchers, Ought to Be A Way To Be a Whole People,* and winner of the Best Play of the Festival award *On the Hills of Black America.*

Storm E has also performed short stories and his original poetry while touring with the Karamu Theater Outreach Performance Series. In addition, he was the opening act for a 40 city tour with Michael Baisden, author of <u>Love, Lust, & Lies</u> and <u>Men Cry in the Dark</u>.

A very moving performance of his poem … *Denied* made Storm E a two time winner of *Showtime at the Apollo.* He has also performed on the *Keenon Ivory Wayans' Show.*

It has been said that watching him perform his poetic works is like watching a storm brewing. According to Desmond, stories+ poems= storms. Visit mrstorme.com and youtube.com to see how he now uses the short film genre as his most recent storytelling medium. His poem, *Twas the Night Before Our Eviction (Refugees of the Economy)* as well as his Apollo performances can be found on these sites. Kommon Knowledge even appears in a short film project of his entitled *Protect & Serve.*

Storm E is the author of a book of poems entitled <u>Assemblage Points</u>. He enjoys reading stories to preschools and elementary children to inspire a desire to enjoy reading within them. He is often a featured poet & speaker to countless schools, community centers, fundraising events, and rallies presenting speeches and poetry that promote self-awareness and social change. *"In the space between my heart, mind, and soul exists a fire that is only extinguished when I release the contents in the form of the spoken word."*

Henry Griffith, Jr. has been writing since he was a young child. He was born in Dayton, OH but grew up in Columbus, OH. He studied Electronic Media Arts at the University of Cincinnati and graduated with a Bachelor of Fine Arts in 2002. For the past seven years, he has been a production assistant at the CBS affiliate in Cincinnati. He was honored in 2005 for his work producing vignettes that aired daily during Black History Month. Since then he has continued to produce those vignettes each year during Black History Month because he believes it is important to highlight the vast history that Cincinnati has contributed to the African-American community.

In 2008, Henry decided to also pursue his lifelong aspiration by starting his own production company, Hentertainment Media. This company provides video production that combines visual graphics to obtain that premium professional look.

With Hentertainment Media, he has been able to highlight that "underground" current that pumps through the Cincinnati nightlife. As the official videographer for the Cincinnati Hip Hop Congress, he has captured a wide range of events such as *Lyrical Insurrection*, *Paint By Numbers*, and *The Beat Lounge Battle*.

His ultimate goal is to make Hentertainment Media a mass media conglomerate centered in its very own studio complex with services ranging from video production, music production and audio production, and major motion picture production. According to Henry: "*I have always found that writing is a tremendous source of release. I am able to transform any emotion into words and make it art as well as relieve stress.*"

Jäe ki-Moja is an eleven year old artist and entrepreneur in Cincinnati, OH. She studies vocal music, visual art, technical theater, and acting. During her spare time she enjoys traveling, drawing Manga characters, fashion designing, and developing her own line of dolls called Jäe Couture. She also helps her father run the online marketplace they established in the spirit of ujaama at artfxafrocentrics.vpweb.com.

Kommon Knowledge is an educator, artist, and activist who resides in Cincinnati, OH. He is a tireless advocate for all forms of grassroots activism on the local level as well as on national fronts. Known by some as Khamin abu-Jäe, he is the proud father of poet Jäe ki-Moja. Poet Shawqui Y. Novoa is his aunt.

The poetry of Kommon Knowledge has been characterized as socially conscious and politically charged. His words are radical and anti-establishment in as much as being pro-revolutionary.

Over the years he has stood shoulder to shoulder with the Peoples Organization for Progress, held down the shouting line with MoveOn in speaking out against the war in Iraq, and marched on the U.S. Justice Department with the National Action Network. His presence is common place in community meetings as well as courthouses, libraries, and anywhere else that the People are gathering.

Kommon Knowledge is the author of two poetry books, <u>As WE Proceed: A Movement for the People</u> & <u>From Protest to Empowerment: Manifesto X & O</u>. He also recorded a spoken word CD of his poems at Creative Soundz Studio entitled *Enemy ME*. His music CD entitled *4 the People* has been called "a soundtrack to the Revolution". Kommon Knowledge has recited his poetry at *The Vibe, Lyrical Insurrection*, and other open mic events. He has appeared in the same venue as DJ King Britt and shared the same microphone as Umar Bin Hassan of the Last Poets. In addition, he produces the *Quiet Storm* neosoul mix CD series as DJ Good 2 Go; widely popular in underground music circles throughout Chicago, St. Louis, Cleveland, and Atlanta.

As an educator, Kommon Knowledge has enjoyed sharing the gift of writing with the scores of children that he has taught in the inner-city Cincinnati schools since 1993. In addition, he empowers a group of teen-aged writers' minds to change the world one word at a time through his work at the InkTank World Headquarters. He also teaches Black history to another group of teens in the Sankofa Educational Enrichment Program. He sees doing these things merely as other ways of furthering his activism and efforts to improve his community. As Khamin puts it: "***A Black man with nothing to prove, has nothing to lose; nothing to lose but his chains … nothing to prove except that he can change … and nothing to change except the game***."

Basil Mustafa was born in Covington, KY. Upon graduation from high school, he attended Sinclair Community College in Dayton, OH in 1985 for basketball and commercial arts. In 1987, He transferred to University of Maryland Eastern Shore and continued his studies and athletics. In 1993, Basil explored his artistic side in the rap group, X-Nation. The group recorded a CD entitled *The X Has Cometh* and performed with Professor Grif of Public Enemy, E.U., Spirit, Tony Terry, The Last Poets, Kamau "The Afro Cat", Steve Cokely and many others. The group was very involved in the Black community influencing awareness of self and improvement throughout Covington, Cincinnati, and Columbus. In 1996, he attended Cincinnati College of Barbering and has been a barber in Cincinnati, Ohio ever since. Basil continues to push himself as an artist by writing and acting. Recently, he appeared in a series pilot by Kole Black entitled *OTR*. In addition, he has continued to serve the community through his work in adult and child rehabilitation programs. And he has also helped coach the Northern Kentucky Tar Heels AAU basketball team. One of Basil's passions is to see "***positive development of minds, bodies and souls in the Black community***."

Shawqui Y. Novoa resides in Philadelphia, PA. She is completing her first book of poetry entitled <u>Inside Me</u>. When she writes, Shawqui often draws upon her life experiences and the people she meets for subject matter. Her earliest experiences with writing provided Shawqui Y. Novoa release as she dealt with separation, death, and financial woes. She came into her own as a poet during the early days of the legendary *Black Lily Sessions* which also helped give rise to fellow Philadelphians Jill Scott, Ursula Rucker, Jaguar Wright, Kindred the Family Soul, and the Jazzyfatnastees, to name a few. She is the mother of poet Ali Bilal. "***Writing for me, in many instances, is a process that starts in pain, chaos, and darkness, but ends in the sunshine and in places that make sense and help heal my emotional wounds and physical pains. And the writing you find in the pages of this book is my further attempt to understand my journey though life. Hopefully, others will find things here that will help them in their journey of pain and joy.***"

Apollos Ra is from St. Louis, MO. At an early age, he discovered spoken word as a way of expressing social consciousness. Through education and life, his awareness of social issues, the plight of the Black race, insight on Black love, and scrutiny of race related matters were enhanced. As a result, Apollos Ra now comfortably exists between the worlds of teaching in the inner-city and completing his doctoral studies at an area university. His views are "***not just those of a Black man; they are ones of an educated man on how issues affect the world, the United States, and especially Black Americans.***"

Darren Reed is an educator and writer who lives in Northern, VA. He has served for 17 successful years as a teacher and principal in inner-city, at-risk school communities. At both levels, Reed has earned numerous recognitions for his accomplishments.

As a principal, Darren Reed created instructional and social development programs aimed to meet the needs at-risk youth. In 2003, Reed designed and coordinated the *Boys to Men Mentoring and Role Model Program*, a comprehensive school-based program designed to assist young boys with their development into adulthood and promote academic success by pairing struggling elementary male students with community role models and mentors and included community service projects, speaker series, tutoring, etc. The program was replicated by other schools and organizations leading to the creation of similar programs for girls.

In 2008, Reed joined K12, Inc. where he helped develop their virtual school delivery model and formed the best practices of serving at-risk students. Reed has since been promoted to Northern Region Vice President at K12, Inc. where he oversees the operations of schools in seven states.

Darren Reed is also a doctoral candidate conducting research on interventions for at-risk students attending a virtual High School in Pennsylvania.

He published his first poetry book, <u>Coco Ways: A Tribute to African American Women</u> in 1999. In addition, Reed's poems have been featured in six volumes of poetry and a host of literary magazines. He has also gained notoriety from performing on the poetry circuit in the DC, VA, and MD area.

Jennifer 'Jai' Washington has spent most of her life living, learning, and loving Cincinnati, OH where she is a recognized entrepreneur, journalist, publisher, and PR/promotions person. She is the director of a nonprofit literary organization which offers a wide range of programming from basic literacy training to advanced creative writing workshops called the InkTank World Headquarters. In 2006, she started EDP Entertainment, LLC. The name is an abbreviation for Every Day People and EDP Entertainment, LLC is an entity dedicated to engaging market forces and focusing them on to the common man and woman because their buying power is often underestimated. One way that Jennifer 'Jai' Washington accomplishes this is through Cincinnati's Conscience (CsC), an *e*Newsletter that she established to bring greater notoriety to her city's thriving underground community of visual and spoken word artist, producers, and musicians. She does this in collaboration with the Cincinnati business community who benefits by advertising with CsC. She promotes herself and her neighborhood contemporaries as products of the Cincinnati brand. Like the city itself, Jennifer 'Jai' Washington describes herself as "*where 'hippie meets hood' and a little of everything in between.*"

Nicole Williams is a native of Cleveland, OH. She is the mother of one and currently working on her first book of poetry, <u>As I Am: A Work In Progress</u>. She has self-published two chapter books, <u>All I Have Is My Words, vol. I & II</u>. She is the recipient of the 2005 Prysmatic Dreams Poet of the Year Award given in Greenville, SC. During that year her poetry received recognition through a CD released by the International House of Poets and produced by DownLow Entertainment entitled *Soulful Branches: Words & Sounds*. That same year she received an award from The Fifth Annual Institute of Freedom Studies for her poem "Mis-education of the N.I.G.G.A" and poem "Ghetto

Serenade: A Sestina" was published in Northern Kentucky University's literary magazine NKU Expressed. The following year her poem "Evolution" was also published in that same magazine.

Nicole's poetry has also appeared on the popular *Whispered Words Poetry* mixtapes: *Mis-education of the N.I.G.G.A (Words Worth & Conspiracy Mix), Things Fall Apart - (Lost Loves Mix), Freestyle ft. Maximus Parthas (Max Mix), Love Like That (Girl Talk Mix).* Coined the Queen of Poetry by her peers and members of The New Word Order, Nicole, whose stage name is NuEshe (meaning new Life) has a brand of poetry all her own. It's a literate blend of Hip Hop intelligence and precisely performed social consciousness that her audience loves.

She has helped produce venues like *The New Word Order National Net Slam* and the celebrated *New Word Order Reach Back Interviews*, which featured The Last Poets. NuEshe has shared the stage with national & international artists like the 2005 Prysmatic Dreams Best New Artist Nyne Elementz and she has opened for The Last Poets, the Def Poetry Jam All Stars, Georgia Me, Malik Salaam, and Kimotion on their *Liquid Lounge Tour.*

NuEshe has blessed the mic at The Secret Society's *Vibe Sessions, The Ra Sessions,* The Legacy's *Love Jones Thursdays* and other poetry venues. She is a chief administrator at one of the internet's hottest poetry lounges, www.prysmaticdreams.com. As one of the founding members of The New Word Order, she helped to organize and promote the major radio broadcast event: **"An Interview with the Fifth Element Live"**, a group of poets comprised of Breeze, Tehut 9, Aqyil, muMs of HBO's *OZ* series, and Jessica Care Moore of *Spoken.* She believes, *"spoken word artists speak for those without a voice... in this business, education should always stand before the entertainment aspect. You don't have to change the pitch in your voice to be heard or use words that the average audience would have to carry a dictionary around to understand what you are talking about; your message should ring loud and clear. Poetry is not about using big words and trying to make yourself seem intelligent, it's about relating to your audience and getting them to think about your message."*

Author's Note

Writing <u>Until Uhuru: For US Colored Folks</u> has truly been a labor of love for me. The pages that you hold are the embodiment of my passions for writing and art along with my desire to elevate and uplift my People. This has been the most ambitious project that I have ever undertaken. Because the message that I needed to convey was such an important one, I called upon many of the gods and earths orbiting within my u-n-I-verse to help me say what needed to be said. Some of these writers I grew up with. Other writers were merely acquaintances that I had made along my quest called knowledge. Still, some of these writers were more like family to me. And a few of them are actual members of my family.

Perhaps it is a bit of an understatement to describe working with 17 other writers as ambitious. With each artist's mentality also came the respective quirks and nuances of dealing with her or him. I am no different. I would often catch mid-day creative vibes and just start writing. Or I would stay up late at night writing because when my 3rd eye is wide awake, I am unable to sleep. Although this is how I would work, I had to learn that sometimes my own creativity had to be put on hold in order to allow each artist the needed time to work in a manner of his or her own choosing.

However, detaching at times in this way was difficult because I had formed an almost symbiotic relationship with this book as I worked to bring it into fruition. Because I put so much of myself into the words and images within, I could no more detach from making this book become a reality than the moon could separate itself from orbiting the planet earth. Like a true movement of uhuru, each of the writers has united within our shared message presented to you on these pages. Though WE have now become one, my People are diverse so the spirit of uhuru here is dynamic. Each of us will continue on from here with our respective works; perhaps collaborating at times within varying combinations and uniting with others to spread our message to the

People. Further, by reading <u>Until Uhuru: For US Colored Folks</u>, you have now united with US as well. You must carry our message with you as you go forth and share it with others and work to better our communities in accordance to one or more of the five tenets upheld in our message. I bid you all peace and blessings. Selah.